DONNA DEWBERRY'S
Designs for
Entertaining

DONNA DEWBERRY'S
Designs for
Entertaining

NORTH LIGHT BOOKS
CINCINNATI, OHIO
www.artistsnetwork.com

Published by North Light Books, an imprint of F+W Publications, Inc., 4700 E. Galbraith Rd., Cincinnati, Ohio, 45236. (800) 289-0963. First edition.

10 09 08 07 06   5 4 3 2 1

Distributed in Canada by Fraser Direct, 100 Armstrong Avenue, Georgetown, ON, Canada L7G 5S4 Tel: (905) 877-4411

Distributed in the U.K. and Europe by David & Charles, Brunel House, Newton Abbot, Devon, TQ12 4PU, England, Tel: (+44) 1626 323200, Fax: (+44) 1626 323319, Email: mail@davidandcharles.co.uk

Distributed in Australia by Capricorn Link, P.O. Box 704, S. Windsor NSW, 2756 Australia, Tel: (02) 4577-3555

Library of Congress Cataloging-in-Publication Data

Dewberry, Donna S.
   Donna Dewberry's designs for entertaining / Donna Dewberry.
       p. cm.
   Includes index.
   ISBN-13: 978-1-58180-802-5 (hardcover : alk. paper)
   ISBN-10: 1-58180-802-X (hardcover : alk. paper)
   ISBN-13: 978-1-58180-799-8 (pbk. : alk. paper)
   ISBN-10: 1-58180-799-6 (pbk. : alk. paper)
  1. Painting--Technique. 2. Decoration and ornament. I. Title: Designs for entertaining. II. Title.
   TT385.D483 2006
   642'.8--dc22

2005027221

Editors: Kathy Kipp and Gina Rath
Production Coordinator: Greg Nock
Designer: Clare Finney
Interior Layout: Kathy B ergstrom
Photographers: Tim Grondin, Al Parrish and Christine Polomsky
Photo stylist: Jan Nickum

Metric Conversion Chart

to convert	to	multiply by
Inches	Centimeters	2.54
Centimeters	Inches	0.4
Feet	Centimeters	30.5
Centimeters	Feet	0.03
Yards	Meters	0.9
Meters	Yards	1.1

About the Author

Donna Dewberry, self-taught artist and creator of the One-Stroke painting technique, has been crafting and decorating for most of her life. Donna is a wife, mother and grand-mother and loves anything to do with painting, crafting, decorating and entertaining.

Donna is a teacher, a very popular painting instructor on PBS television, and author of seven other North Light books. By sharing her talents through these books, Donna hopes to teach and inspire as many people as she can. She hopes that you use this book for many years to develop your own talents and then share them with others.

Donna has her own One-Stroke painting workshop certification classes taught all over the country as well as many other workshops incorporating her One-Stroke technique. Information on all Donna's workshops can be found on her website, www.onestroke.com

Dedication

While creating this book I thought about my daughters and daughters in-law. Like me, each of them loves to share their homes, party ideas, and favorite recipes with family and friends. Each of them has celebrated events complete with festive table decor and deli-cious food. With them in mind I dedicate this book to Maria, Kara, Amanda, Anna, Lynn, and Laurie. Thank you for being an inspiration to me.

Love, Mom

Acknowledgments

I would like to acknowledge all of the people that made this book possible: my editors, Kathy Kipp and Gina Rath, and the photographers, stylists and designers at North Light Books. My staff at Dewberry Designs who make me look so good, especially Maribel, Doris and Althea—without whom this book would not have come together.

Grateful thanks to Donna Provalenko at Springs Industries and seamstress Nancy Newell for creating several gorgeous table linens for this book! Your fabric placemats, napkins, hot pads and table runner have added a lovely finishing touch to the photos of the table settings.

I would also like to acknowledge my husband Marc, who always encourages me, helps to bring things into perspective and keeps me focused. Without him in my life I know that none of this would have been possible. I truly believe that our Heavenly Father sur-rounds us with people who fill the voids in our lives; Marc has completed me.

contents

Supplies and Basic Techniques

Donna's Designs for Entertaining

supplies and basic techniques

About One-Stroke Painting

Congratulations on taking the first steps! One-Stroke painting is a fast and easy form of decorative painting. It is a great stepping stone to get you started in a wonderful and stress-free hobby. Who knows? You might even be able to make a career out of it!

Here are a couple of things to keep in mind as you are learning.

Give yourself time to learn and practice. You will only get better with practice. Don't be discouraged; everyone has to start somewhere. Every time you paint something, it will look better than the time before.

Learning to paint is like learning to walk; you had to crawl before you could stand, and you had to stand before you could walk. The same holds true for decorative painting. You have to develop muscle-memory to be able to hold the brush handle straight up and down—which is the proper way for painting the One Stroke technique. Everyone is used to holding a pen or a pencil tilted. For painting, you will grip the brush the same as a pencil, but instead of tilting the handle, you will need to keep it upright. You'll also learn how to load your brush properly. Loading means getting the paint on the brush in a controlled amount for painting (see Loading the Flat Brush on page 14).

Begin by becoming familiar with the brushes you'll be using. Here is some helpful information for you to keep in mind as you learn the One-Stroke method of painting.

Bigger is Better

When first learning One-Stroke painting, you'll find that larger brushes (such as a 3/4-inch (19mm) flat and a no. 12 flat) are easier to control than smaller brushes. Avoid using small brushes until you are comfortable with the loading process and the strokes. Many people think smaller brushes are easier to control; while this may be true for other painting techniques, it is not true when learning One Stroke. With One Stroke, you use a double loaded brush most of the time, and when you use larger brushes it is easier to see the strokes as you make them. Always vary the brush size depending on the size surface you are painting.

Telltale Bristles. The bristles of your brush can help you when learning the One-Stroke technique. They will tell you if you are tilting the handle too much during a stroke. They will also tell you if you are twisting the brush instead of wiggling when painting a shell stroke. The bristles need to follow the ferrule (the metal part) of the brush. Things to watch for:

- If you see the bristles out to the side of the ferrule, then you are probably tilting the handle to the side.

- If during a shell stroke the bristles start to pass up the ferrule, then you are twisting the brush instead of wiggling.

- At the end of the stroke when you lift up to the chisel edge, if you see a slight bend to the bristles then you are not all the way up on the chisel edge. Lifting the brush off of the surface before coming all the way up on the chisel will result in a "feathered" ending to the stroke. This is caused by the bristles "flicking" as the brush is lifted up.

- While learning, keep your eye on the bristles; you'll find that as you become more experienced, mistakes will disappear.

Brushes

One Stroke brushes are available in several shapes, sizes and types. For the projects in this book, we will be using specific types of brushes depending on the specific paint being used. Examples of brushes for regular acrylic paints are shown at right.

Flats. Painting the One-Stroke technique requires the use of flat brushes. One Stroke flat brushes are designed with longer bristles and less thickness in the bodies of the bristles to allow for a much sharper chisel edge. A sharp chisel edge is essential to the success of the One-Stroke technique, as most of the strokes begin and end on the chisel edge.

Scruffy Brushes. The scruffy brush that I have created is ready to be used straight out of the package. All you have to do is "fluff the scruff" as we say. Remove the brush from the packaging and form the natural hair bristles into an oval shape by gently pulling on them. Then, twist the bristles in the palm of your hand until you have a nice oval shape. Now you are ready to pounce into paint and begin.

When fluffed, the scruffy brush is used for painting mosses, wisteria, lilacs, hair and fur, and even for faux finishing and shading textures. Do not use water when painting with this brush.

To clean the scruffy brush, pounce the bristles into the brush basin. Do not rake them across the ribs in the basin or you will break the natural hair bristles.

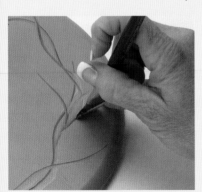

Liner Brushes. There are two sizes of liner brushes. The no. 1 script liner (sometimes referred to as the mini) is usually used for small detail work where more control is needed. The no. 2 script liner is used where less control is needed.

The liner brush is used with paint of an "inky" consistency. See page 16 for how to load the liner brush.

Clean these brushes as you do the flat brushes. Be gentle, but clean thoroughly.

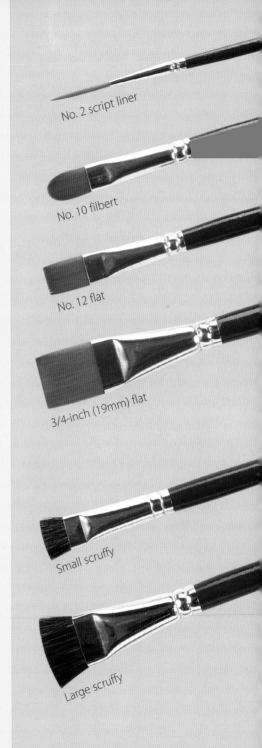

No. 2 script liner

No. 10 filbert

No. 12 flat

3/4-inch (19mm) flat

Small scruffy

Large scruffy

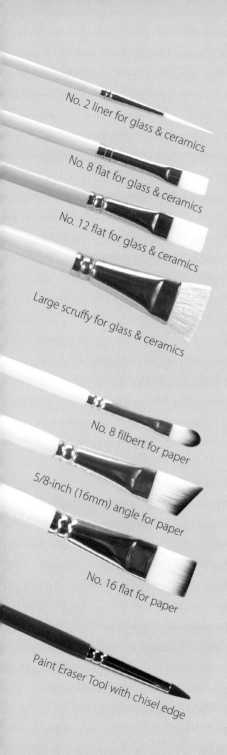

No. 2 liner for glass & ceramics

No. 8 flat for glass & ceramics

No. 12 flat for glass & ceramics

Large scruffy for glass & ceramics

No. 8 filbert for paper

5/8-inch (16mm) angle for paper

No. 16 flat for paper

Paint Eraser Tool with chisel edge

Angle Brushes. An angle brush is similar to a flat brush. The only difference is that the chisel edge is trimmed at an angle, making one side longer (toe) than the other side (heel). The One Stroke angle brush is specifically developed to work with the One Stroke painting technique; these brushes feature clean, chiseled edges to create crisp, accurate strokes. The angle brush is designed to make creating comma strokes, which are used in many of my designs, much easier.

Filbert Brushes. A filbert brush is a flat brush with a chiseled edge that has been cut in a curve. One Stroke filbert brushes are specifically designed to work with the One Stroke painting technique to produce accurate, beautiful oval-shaped strokes.

This brush creates a rounder outer edge on the petals of flowers such as a daisy, chrysanthemum and lilac.

Round Brushes. The One Stroke round brush is very versatile. It can be used to make scrolls, flower petals, leaves, and letters. It holds a lot of paint and the roundness eliminates sharp edges, making elegant strokes easy. When lettering, thinning the paint slightly will allow you to paint a lot of letters before needing to reload. By using pressure you can make thick strokes; by easing the pressure and lifting to the tip, you can make thinner strokes. This brush can be double loaded or multi-loaded. The bristles can also be pressed against the surface and flared out, then pulled back and lifted to make an awesome tulip petal!

Lettering Brushes. The One Stroke lettering brush is similar to the flat brush but has longer bristles that hold more paint, which is very helpful when lettering. Another difference is the three-sided contour handle; this handle creates the perfect hand positioning for beautiful lettering. These brushes are specifically designed to work with the One Stroke painting technique to produce accurate, beautiful results.

Glass and Ceramic Brushes. Developed for use with FolkArt Enamels, these brushes feature softer bristles and allow for smooth paint application on slick, reflective and nonporous surfaces such as glass, tile, china and ceramics.

One Stroke Outdoor Basecoating Brushes. These large, thick brushes are specifically designed to apply paint smoothly and evenly over large areas. Polyester bristles provide durability for use on outdoor projects. They come in a 1-1/2 inch (3.8cm) flat and a 2-inch (5.1cm) angle.

One Stroke Brushes for Paper Surfaces. Stiffer bristles make these brushes ideal for painting on paper with thick FolkArt Papier Paint.

Paints and Mediums

We will be using a variety of paints and mediums in this book. To achieve the expected results, it's important to use the specific medium with the paint for which it was made; don't mix mediums.

FolkArt Acrylic Colors. Plaid FolkArt Acrylic Colors are high-quality bottled acrylic paints. Their rich and creamy formulation and long open time make them perfect for decorative painting. They are offered in a wide range of wonderful premixed colors and in gleaming metallic shades.

FolkArt Artists' Pigments. Artists' Pigments are pure colors that are perfect for mixing your own shades. Their intense colors and creamy consistencies are wonderful for blending, shading and highlighting. Because they're acrylic paints, they're easy to clean up.

FolkArt Enamels. Enamels are the ultimate one-step, dishwasher-safe paints for glass and ceramics. These revolutionary paints are highly pigmented and go on rich and creamy. FolkArt Enamels make project care a breeze—painted pieces will maintain their rich color, even when washed on the top rack of your dishwasher. There are a few general instructions for using Enamels Paints:

- Always clean glass surfaces with rubbing alcohol to remove dirt and oils. Be careful not to touch the areas you are painting as your fingers will leave a trace of skin oils on the glass.

- Always follow the manufacturer's instructions for baking and washing the painted surface.

- Do not use in direct contact with food. And never cut on a surface that has been painted. Reverse painting on the back of glass plates is recommended if the plate is to be used for food.

- Don't use water to thin Enamels; use only Flow Medium to moisten the bristles and to thin the paint. And use the Flow Medium only with the liner brushes, fan brushes or rake brushes. Do not thin the consistency of the paint when using any of the other brushes such as flats or angle brushes.

If you are painting a stroke of Enamels paint on top of an existing stroke, there are a few things that you need to keep in mind.

- If the paint of the first stroke is completely wet or completely dry, then painting a stroke on top will give you satisfactory results.

- If the paint is partially wet (such as having one edge that is thicker), then painting a stroke over that one will cause the wet parts of the first stroke to lift, resulting in undesirable splotches of thin and thick paint.

- To avoid this problem, allow any strokes that will be overlapped to completely dry before painting over them. Use a blow dryer to quicken the drying process if needed.

All Enamels painting must be completed within 24 hours of starting a project. Any paint applied after 24 hours or after baking will not fuse properly and will not have the same durability during washing. So any piece painted dimensionally will need to be hand washed rather than placed in the dishwasher.

Outdoor Acrylics. The new Outdoor paints can be used on a variety of surfaces: unpainted or painted metal, tin, terra cotta, wood, stone and concrete. Outdoor paint is made with a sealer in it. It has been lab tested to withstand normal weather conditions equivalent to 3-5 years. Do not mix water with this paint. Water will dilute the sealer and reduce durability.

You can use Outdoor paint two ways, with a brush or straight from the bottle with a tip. Currently there are 38 opaque colors and 8 metallic colors available in 2 oz. (59ml) bottles, and 8 opaque colors and 2 metallic colors available in dimensional bottles. You can use regular acrylic brushes or brushes made for paper.

Tips on Using Enamels and Outdoor Paints.

When using these paints straight from the bottle for dimensional embellishments:

- Hold the bottle just slightly above the surface and give even pressure to the bottle as you outline or embellish.

- Try to work with the tip of the bottle ahead of the paint, holding the bottle at a slight angle like a pen or pencil.

- Pull the lines rather than push through the paint. Pulled strokes look much nicer and are easier to execute than pushed strokes.

- Make sure to lift the bottle straight up as you exit from a line and watch to be sure the paint has separated from the bottle.

- Wipe the tip of the bottle if you notice a buildup of paint.

Lettering can also be done straight from the bottle. The bottle tip can be used to write or draw just like a pencil or pen. If you want to make finer lines, use one of the metal tips from the Tip-Pen Set (see page 13) and screw it directly onto the bottle. Make sure to drop the metal tip into water after use to prevent the paint from drying and clogging the tip.

If you are embellishing with two colors next to each other, keep in mind that if you get the two colors too close, the paint will flow together. This can also happen when making dots. Experiment and see just how close is "too close." Sometimes you may want the colors to flow together. But if you want your accents to be separate, be sure to keep the colors separated.

You can always dry the first color a bit with a blow dryer.

If using a blow dryer or a heat gun, do not overheat the dimensional embellishments. If you do, the paint will form little bubbles that pop—ruining the dimensional effect.

It is very important to wipe the tip of the dimensional paint bottle before replacing the cap. Paint can build up in the cap, causing the tip of the bottle to bend.

FolkArt Papier Paints. This specially formulated paint for paper crafting is perfect for stroke work, backgrounds and adding dimension to painted projects. It is acid free and non-blocking. This means it's great for memory album and scrapbooking projects and won't stick to other surfaces once it is dry. Plus it is flexible, which means it won't crack and flake as papers bend.

Mediums

Floating Medium. Specially formulated for "floating" acrylic colors, this gel won't run as water can, and it dries quickly without extenders. I also use it to make my acrylic colors more transparent and to float shadows or shading.

Flow Medium. FolkArt Enamels Flow Medium thins regular Enamels paints for shading and easy line work. Painted glass pieces will maintain their rich color, even when washed on the top rack of your dishwasher.

Clear Medium. Enamels Clear Medium is used with the double loaded brush technique to achieve just the right paint consistency for effects such as shadows and shading. It also creates transparent effects without compromising the paint's adhesion. See page 15 for more information.

Tools

Enamels Detail Painters. These tools are very versatile. Their rounded sponge ends can be used to apply paint when stenciling a design or to create perfect little dots to make grapes, berries or simply a dotted surface (see below).

One Stroke Paint Eraser Tool. Use the hard rubber-tipped eraser tool to wipe away excess paint and to create precise fine detail or to dot in the centers of flowers (see photo page 10).

Enamels Tip-Pen Set. These tips fit onto any bottle of Enamels paint so that the paint can be squeezed directly from the bottle to create fine lines. The set includes both plastic and metal tips (see below).

One Stroke Adhesive Background Templates. These templates come in a variety of designs for stencilling in motifs to fill in background areas of your projects. Use them on any surface. Shown at right is the template for ovals.

One Stroke Palette. The FolkArt One Stroke Paint Palette that I use is a durable and handy palette that allows you to keep paint and tools at your fingertips. The circular palette has numerous paint wells, holes for brushes and a place for paper towels. The palette is designed for left or right handed usage and holds a 9-inch (23cm) disposable foam plate.

What I especially like about the palette is the comfort. There is no need to grip the palette as it is designed to balance comfortably on your hand. And when the foam plate gets filled up with paint colors, just pull it out of the tabs and throw it away.

Brush Caddy. The One Stroke Brush Caddy holds your brushes while you paint and also cleans the paint out of the bristles. Rake the brush along the ribs in the bottom of the water basin to help dislodge the paint, then store the brush in one of the holes along the side to dry.

Loading the Flat Brush

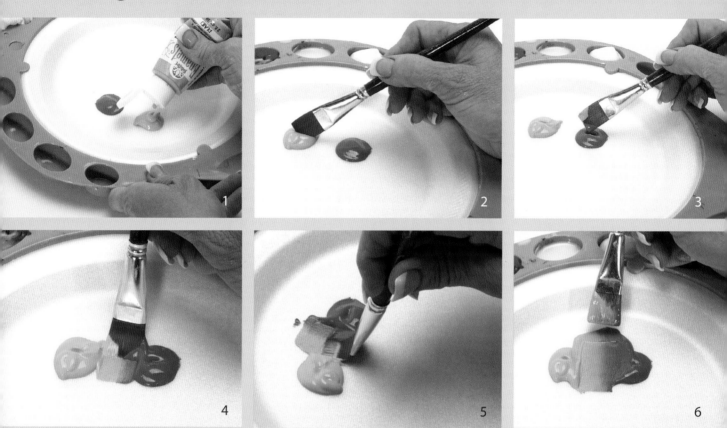

Double Loading a Flat Brush

1. Pour two puddles of paint on the foam plate on your palette. Space the puddles a little bit wider than the width of the brush you will be loading. Moisten the bristles of your brush with clean water and blot on a paper towel to remove the excess moisture.

2. Dip one corner of the bristles into the lighter color. Make sure the brush is angled when you dip it into the paint.

3. Now dip the other corner of the bristles into the second puddle of paint.

4. Begin to work a "track" between the two puddles of paint by touching on the chisel edge and stroking it back, pushing down hard against the palette.

5. This photo shows how hard I'm pushing down on the brush so that the metal ferrule almost touches the palette. Now pull in a straight line about 1-1/2-inches (3.8cm) long. Lift the brush at the end of the track, lay the bristles down so that the other side of the bristles are touching the plate and then push and pull back to the starting point.

6. Stroke back and forth about four times and then pick up more paint on each corner and work the brush in the track again. Continue to do this until the paint is worked into the bristles about two-thirds of the way up towards the ferrule. You will know that the brush is fully loaded when it feels like you are painting with softened butter. If the brush feels like it is "dragging," then you need more paint on the brush.

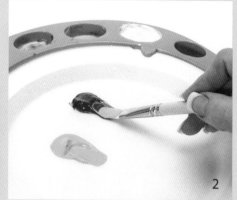

Double Loading a Filbert Brush

1. Load one flat side of the brush with your first color by placing the brush on the edge of the paint puddle and pulling paint out.

2. Turn the brush over and load the other flat side with the second color in the same way.

Sideloading a Flat or Filbert

3. Begin by moistening the bristles of your brush in water then blotting on a paper towel to remove excess moisture. Fully load your brush with a medium by touching the chisel edge to the edge of the puddle, push-ing down to flatten the bristles, then pulling away from the puddle. Lift the brush and repeat. Flip the brush over and work the medium into the other side of the bristles. Work the medium into the brush until it is two thirds of the way towards the ferrule.

4. To sideload, pull your medium-loaded brush through one edge of the paint puddle so the color extends only partway across the bristles. If needed, you can sideload a sec-ond color by tipping into the edge of the puddle of the second color.

How to Use Mediums

When using Floating Medium, Clear Medium or Flow Medium, fully load your brush with paint prior to adding any medium (see page 14). To load medium, dip the chisel edge of a fully-loaded brush straight into and straight out of the puddle of medium as shown above, and then work it into the brush using the same method that was used to load the brush. It is recom-mended that you pick up medium only about every second or third stroke. Mediums should not be used in place of a fully-loaded brush. Too much medium will turn the colors transparent or will cause the colors to blend too much and become a "muddy" color.

Loading the Script Liner

1. The script liner is used with paint that has been thinned. Use water to thin Acrylic paints; use the Enamels Flow Medium to thin the Enamels paints; use the Papier Flow Medium to thin the Papier paints, and the Outdoor Flow Medium to thin the Outdoor paints. The different mediums are not interchangeable; they each have special properties that make them compatible with their specific paints. Load the script liner by first dipping the bristles into the appropriate thinner on your palette.

2. Lay the bristles down next to a puddle of paint. Start to move the liner in a small circle allowing the tips of the bristles to touch the edge of the puddle of paint. Go back and pick up more of the thinner and continue to make the circles, repeating three times until you see an ink-like (or "inky") consistency.

3. Once you have reached the correct consistency, pull the brush out from the puddle and drag it on the plate while you twist the brush in your finger tips and lift to the tip. You should see a nice point at the tip of the brush.

4. Use this loading method with two kinds of brushes: liners and dagger brushes.

Painting a One-Stroke Leaf

1. Double load a flat brush with a lighter and darker color. Here I'm using two shades of green, but you can paint leaves in almost any colors you want. Begin on the chisel edge, then push down on the bristles. Keep your eye on the dark edge as you form the shape of the leaf.

2. Turn the dark side of the bristles towards the tip of the leaf.

3. Then lift back up to the chisel edge before you lift the brush from the surface. The last part of the brush to lift off is the light side of the bristles.

4. Pull a stem partway into the leaf using just the chisel edge of the brush.

1

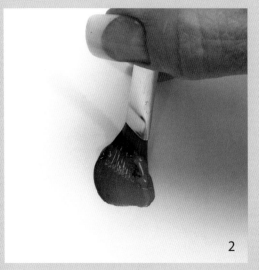

2

3

4

17

Painting a Heart-shaped Leaf

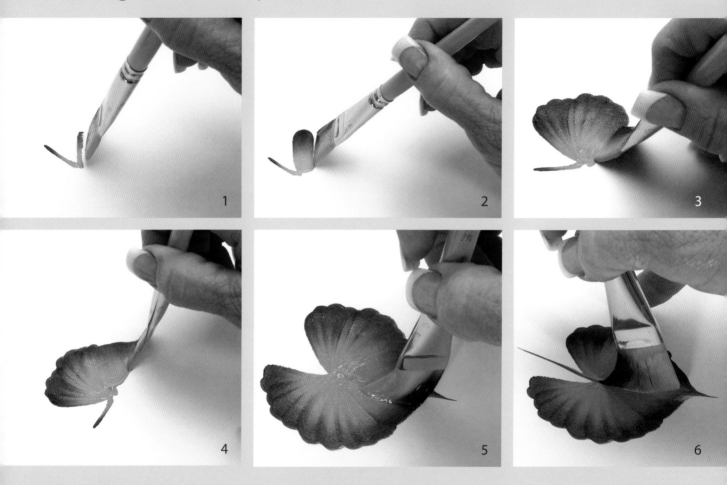

Heart-shaped Leaf

1. Double load a flat brush with two shades of green. With the brush's chisel edge, make a V on your surface.

2. Begin at one side of the V with a starter stroke: push down and lift, repeating three times (this starter stroke is very important!).

3. After the third starter stroke, push down and begin to wiggle the bristles back and forth. You'll begin to see a "sea shell" shape.

4. Lift and slide evenly up to the chisel.

5. Turn the brush over so the darker green is to the outside. Repeat on the other side. Notice how the handle of the brush is standing straight up and down.

6. Pull a stem halfway into the leaf (only halfway), leading with the light color and staying up on the chisel.

Smooth-Sided and Chisel-Edge Leaves

Smooth-Sided Leaf

1. Double load a flat brush and paint one half of a leaf following Steps 1-4 on the previous page. The second side of this leaf has a smooth edge. Turn your brush over so the darker green is to the outside. Begin on the chisel, keep your eye on the dark green edge of the brush and touch, slide, then pivot on the lighter green side of the brush.

2. Slide evenly and lift up to the tip. The lighter green side of the brush should lead the way.

1

2

1

2

3

Chisel-Edge Leaf

1. Chisel-edge leaves are quick to paint in one smooth motion. Double load a flat brush with two shades of green. Begin on the chisel, push down lightly.

2. Slide to the tip as you lift back up to the chisel. Be sure you are all the way up on the chisel edge before you lift your brush off the surface, otherwise you will not get a nice sharp leaf tip.

3. Pull a stem partway into the leaf, staying up on the chisel edge and leading with the lighter green side. Do you see how the brush is being held straight up and down, not tilted? This is very important when working with the chisel edge of the bristles.

Ruffled-Edge Leaf and Comma Stroke

Ruffled-Edge Leaf

1. The ruffled edges of this leaf are more irregular than the wiggled edges of a heart-shaped leaf. Double load the brush with two colors such as green and yellow. Keeping your eye on the green side of the brush, wiggle out and slide back in to the center vein. Repeat a few times, then turn the brush, lift to the chisel, and slide to the tip.

2. Repeat for the other half of the leaf, keeping the green to the outside edge. The ruffles on both sides of the leaf do not have to match or line up.

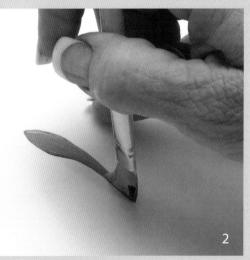

Comma Stroke

1. With a double loaded brush, begin on the chisel edge, then push down until the bristles are bending as you see in the photo.

2. Slide and lift to the tip. Make sure you are all the way up on the chisel edge before you lift the brush off the surface.

3. To make a series of leaves, continue adding more comma strokes on either side of the first one, angling them toward the center to create a stem.

Tip Comma strokes are great for painting all kinds of flower petals and leaves using the chisel edge of a flat brush. Or try comma strokes with a round brush, too.

Holly Leaf and Pine Needles

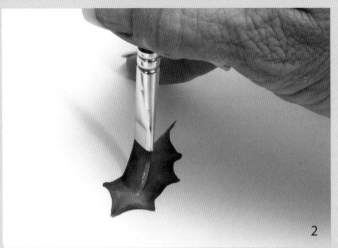

Holly Leaf and Pine Needles

1. Double load a flat brush with two shades of green. Begin on the chisel edge and, keeping the brush straight up and down, slide out to form a point. The darker green side of the brush is to the outside.

2. Slide back in toward the center of the leaf.

3. Continue making two more points on this side of the holly leaf, then turn and slide back up to the tip.

4. Finish by pulling in the stem. To add some pine needles around the leaf, double load your brush with the same two greens. Begin on the chisel, leading with the light green, then pull, lifting up the light green side.

Long Thin Leaf, Vine and Curlicues

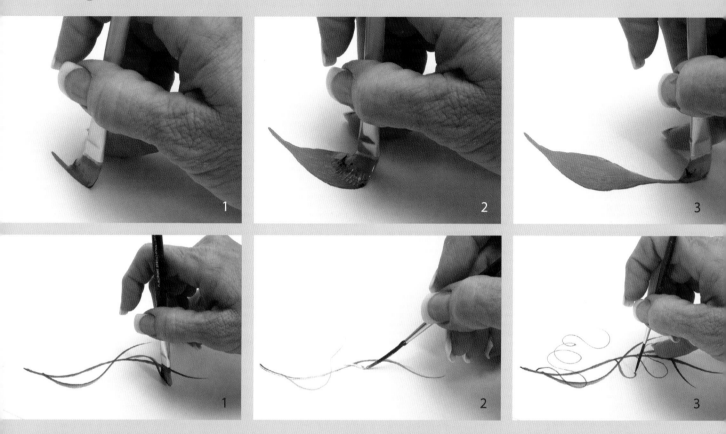

Long, Thin Leaf
This stroke can be used for painting long and narrow leaves, such as you'll find on herbs and some flowers.

1. Double load the brush. Begin on the chisel, and slide.

2. As you pull, press down on the side of the brush.

3. Slide back up to the chisel and pull out a stem.

Painting a Vine with the Chisel Edge
1. Double load the brush. Begin on the chisel edge and lead with the lighter color. Stay up on the chisel edge of your brush using your little finger to balance. Pull each stroke from the main vine.

Painting a Vine with the Script Liner
2. Load the script liner with inky paint (see page 16). Balance with your little finger against the surface, and pull the vines toward you. Make sure each overlapping vine starts at the main vine before curving away and crossing over.

Curlicues
3. Follow the instructions in step 2 above, but hold the brush handle perpendicular to the surface. Brace with your little finger and paint loose, curly lines. Move your whole arm, not just your wrist.

Tip By using a little pressure and then lifting as you slide the liner, you can create delicate butterfly bodies and thin scroll work.

Ribbon with Flat and Liner Brushes

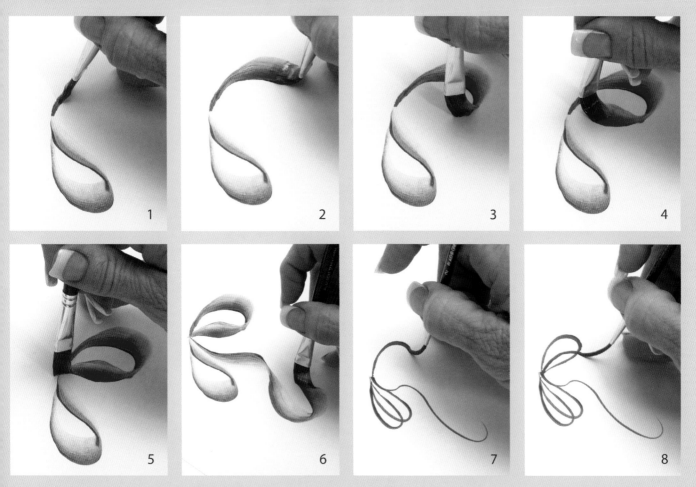

Painting a Ribbon with the Flat Brush

1. We'll start with the first loop already painted so you can see one finished. To paint the second loop, double load a flat brush and begin on the chisel edge.

2. Slide and push down on the bristles.

3. Lift back up to the chisel.

4. Then push down and flatten the bristles the other way.

5. Lift and slide to the tip.

6. Use the same technique to create the ribbon's tail.

Painting a Ribbon with a Script Liner

7. Load a script liner with inky paint (see page 16). Paint a couple of loops and a tail, following the instructions for painting Curlicues on the previous page.

8. Halfway through the first loop, paint another loop, stroking out and back in to the center point. Finish with another tail.

Five-Petal Flowers

1. Double load a flat or angle brush with two colors, or two shades of the same color. Begin on the chisel edge at the base of each petal.

2. Push down on the bristles and curve around.

3. Then lift back up to the chisel. Don't flip your brush over for each new petal—keep the same color to the outside edge. If it's easier, turn your work as you paint each petal. With more practice you'll be able to paint five-petal flowers quickly without turning your surface.

4. Use the handle end of your brush or a Paint Eraser tool to dot in the centers with another color.

1

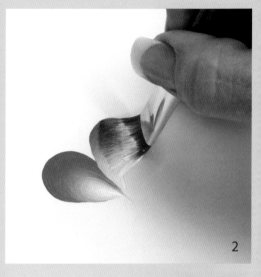

2

3

4

Ruffled-Edge Flower Petals

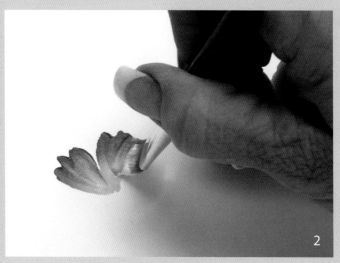

1. Double load a flat brush with two colors, or two shades of the same color. Here I've already painted a petal so you can see and compare. Begin on the chisel edge.

2. Wiggle out and in a few times for each petal, just as you would for a ruffled-edge leaf (see page 20).

3. Then slide back in to the center.

4. Repeat Steps 1-3 for each petal. Turn your surface as you go to make painting easier. When all the petals are complete, use a small Paint Eraser tool to dot in the centers with another color.

Quick Tips

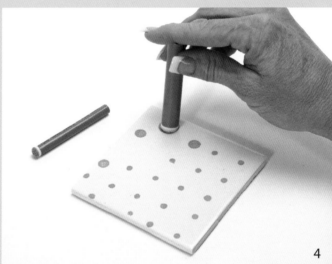

Removing the Top from Papier Paint
1. To squeeze out some Papier Paint onto your palette, you need to pop the top off the bottle and squeeze it onto the palette.

Using the Paint Eraser Tool
2. The One Stroke Paint Eraser Tools are specifically designed with chiseled and tapered points to wipe away excess paint or to create precise, fine detail such as these tiny wildflower petals.

Using an Adhesive Background Template
3. Apply the template to your surface, being sure to smooth it down. Then use a scruffy brush to pounce color onto the surface. Remove the template by lifting straight up.

Detail Painters/Dotters
4. Load by gently placing the tip in paint. Hold perpendicular to the surface, press down and lift straight off.

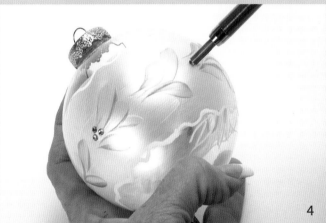

Outlining

You can add dimension and outline two different ways: with the Tip Pen Set, or by using one of the dimensional paints that's right for your surface, such as the Outdoor or Papier paints.

1. To use the Tip Pen Set, remove the top from the paint bottle and replace it with a metal tip. Choose the size tip you want and screw it onto the extension, then apply the paint to the surface.

2. To use one of the dimensional paints, simply remove the cap and apply directly from the bottle. When using the dimensional paints, I find it helpful to apply a little on a scrap piece of paper just so I know how hard I need to squeeze the paint out for the size line that I want.

Applicator Wand

3. To help apply embellishments such as beads, gems or crystals to my painted holiday ornaments, I use the Kandi Kane Applicator Wand, following the manufacturer's instructions.

4. The applicator wand helps position the beads precisely in the right place (see page 67 for a finished ornament).

celebrate the
seasons

Celebrate every season in style. Entertaining doesn't have to be grand or elaborate. By adding your personal touch you will make any party or occasion memorable. Celebrate the beginning of spring or summer by painting a set of everyday china with a pretty wildflower theme. For fall, serve your guests a spicy seasonal bread or coffee cake on a tray painted with colorful fall mums. Make warm memories on a cold winter's night: snuggle up with the little ones in front of a roaring fire and serve hot cocoa from mugs that you painted especially for them. No matter the time of year, there are lots of ideas to choose from. Just look around you and find the beauty in each season!

FolkArt Enamels Paints

- Magenta
- Violet Pansy
- Fresh Foliage
- Thicket
- Hydrangea
- Periwinkle
- Sunflower
- Yellow Ochre
- Wicker White
- Licorice

One Stroke Glass/Ceramics Brushes

- no. 6 flat
- no. 8 flat
- no. 10 flat
- no. 12 flat
- no. 2 script liner

Supplies

- Flow Medium
- Paint Erasers, tapered

Surfaces

- Plain white china plates and clear drinking glasses (available at department and discount stores)

spring into summer

Some of my favorite gardens are wildflower gardens. I love watching the bees busily collecting nectar from the blossom of each wildflower. As the flowers sway and turn in the summer breeze, each one seems to take on a personality of its own.

I have discovered a beautiful and easy way to share my wildflower garden with my friends and family all year long: by painting wildflowers on china!

There are a few important things to remember when using your handpainted china. Even though the paint is non-toxic, it does not meet the requirements to be considered food safe. So place a clear glass plate over your painted china for serving food. On drinking glasses, keep the paint on the outside only.

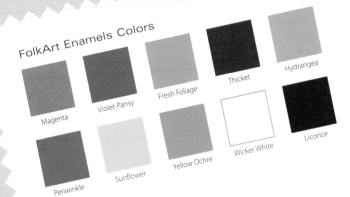

FolkArt Enamels Colors

Magenta Violet Pansy Fresh Foliage Thicket Hydrangea

Periwinkle Sunflower Yellow Ochre Wicker White Licorice

Enamels Colors

Fresh Foliage
Thicket
Yellow Ochre
Sunflower
Wicker White
Violet Pansy
Licorice

Wildflowers and Bees

1. Prepare your white china dinner plate by cleaning with a soft cloth. When deciding where to place your design, look at the height and placement and make sure there is enough space for the leaves and flowers to fit in. Double load a no. 12 flat with Fresh Foliage and Thicket and chisel in the stems.

2. Load a no. 2 script liner with a little Flow Medium and Fresh Foliage. The paint should be an inky consistency so the liner can make tiny lines for the flower stems. Alternate Fresh Foliage and Thicket so your stems are varied in color. Also add the tiny bases at the ends of the flower stems for the petals.

3. Load a no. 12 flat with Fresh Foliage, sideload into a little Thicket and chisel in thin, fern-like leaves.

4. Add enough fern-like leaves to fill in along the stems.

5. Load Fresh Foliage onto the same brush and paint one-stroke leaves onto the second set of stems on the right side of the plate.

6. Add some Thicket to your brush and finish the one-stroke leaves.

7. Double load a tapered Paint Eraser tool with Yellow Ochre and Sunflower and dot on the tiny flower petals. Keep these airy.

8. Load a no. 8 flat into Wicker White, sideload into Violet Pansy, and paint the purple blossoms; wiggle up and slide down.

9. Pull in a few stems to meet the bottoms of the flowers where needed.

10. Using a no. 8 flat double loaded with Fresh Foliage and Thicket, add two large leaves at the bottom of the stems. Paint the first leaf keeping the Thicket to the inside, then flip the brush over and paint the second leaf with the Thicket to the outside.

11. To paint the bees, double load a no. 8 flat with Sunflower and Yellow Ochre. Stroke in the bodies of the bees, using the same stroke as a one-stroke leaf (see page 17).

12. Use the same brush and Wicker White for the wings. Stroke them in just like a couple of one-stroke leaves.

13. Use inky Licorice on a no. 2 script liner to add the short fur on the body. Stay on the tip of the bristles using short, little strokes.

14. Using the same brush and color, outline the wings and add the antennae.

Enamels Colors

Fresh Foliage
Thicket
Wicker White
Magenta
Sunflower

Five-Petal Magenta Flowers

1. Paint the white china dessert plates with these bright magenta flowers. Begin with the large greenery at the bottom. Stroke in the stems using the chisel edge of a no. 10 flat. Paint the large leaves with the same brush, using Fresh Foliage sideloaded with a tiny bit of Thicket. Stroke in the flower stems using a no. 2 script liner and inky Thicket. Add the calyx on the stems with a touch-and-pull stroke.

2. Load a no. 6 flat with Wicker White, sideload with a tiny bit of Magenta and paint the background flower petals using teardrop-shaped strokes.

3. Add more Magenta to the brush and paint the foreground flowers, keeping the Magenta to the outside.

4. Dot the centers with Sunflower using the tapered Paint Eraser tool.

Strawberry Cake

CAKE
  1 box yellow cake mix
  3/4 cup (177 ml) vegetable oil
  1 small pkg. strawberry Jell-O
  1 pkg. frozen strawberries
  4 eggs

ICING
  2-1/2 Tbsp. (22 ml) juice from berries
  1 cup (237 ml) powdered sugar

Mix all cake ingredients and bake at
350° F (175°C) for one hour. Remove
immediately and top with icing.

1

2

3

4

Enamels Colors

Fresh Foliage
Thicket
Yellow Ochre
Sunflower
Wicker White
Periwinkle
Hydrangea

Tall Drinking Glasses

1. Anytime you paint clear glassware, be sure to paint only the outside and keep all paint away from the rim of the glass. To paint the light green leaves and stems on the tall glasses at left, use Fresh Foliage and a no. 10 flat.

2. Add the dark leaves and stems with Thicket using the same brush.

3. Double load a no. 10 flat with Periwinkle and Hydrangea. Leading with the Hydrangea, chisel in the little flower buds.

4. Using the same brush and colors, add the larger flower petals. Dot in yellow flower centers with Sunflower on the tapered paint eraser tool.

Short Glasses

1. Use a no. 10 flat and Fresh Foliage sideloaded with a little Thicket to chisel in the ferns. Paint the body of the bee with Sunflower and Yellow Ochre (see step 11 on page 34).

2. Finish the bee following steps 12-14 on page 34. This is the same bee that was painted on the dinner plates (see photo at right). Repeating parts of the design on different pieces of your dinnerware helps pull them together into a charming and cohesive set.

1

2

fall tray

FolkArt Acrylic Paints
- Linen
- Hauser Green Light
- Thicket
- Burnt Umber
- Vintage White
- Yellow Ochre
- School Bus Yellow
- True Burgundy

FolkArt Metallics
- Inca Gold Metallic

Brushes
- One Stroke Outdoor Basecoating 1-1/2-inch (3.8cm)
- 3/4-inch (19mm) flat
- nos. 12 and 16 flats
- no. 10 filbert
- no. 2 script liner

Supplies
- FolkArt Antiquing Polish (brown)
- Soft white cotton cloth

Surface
- Tray available from Wood-Ware, inc. www.wood-ware.net, 1-239-540-1744

I like to go to garage sales and find old silver trays that are embossed, tarnished and labeled irreparable. I prime the tray with white spray paint, basecoat with whatever color I choose, then finish with the painting process described on the following pages. Embossed edges really add interest to a tray. Once painted, the tray can be given as a gift or used for serving a delicious fall treat.

Vases, candle holders and tureens can also be painted to match, making a nice complete table setting.

Trays of all kinds and sizes are available at department stores, craft supply stores and discount stores.

FolkArt Acrylic Colors

Linen

Hauser Green Light

Thicket

Burnt Umber

Vintage White

FolkArt Metallic

Yellow Ochre

True Burgundy

School Bus Yellow

Inca Gold Metallic

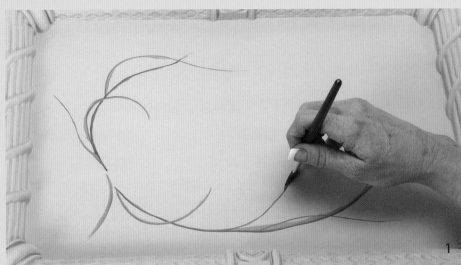

1. Basecoat the tray using Linen and a 1-1/2-inch (3.8cm) Outdoor Basecoating brush; allow to dry completely. Load a 3/4-inch (19mm) flat with Hauser Green Light, Thicket and Burnt Umber to paint the vines. Occasionally pick up a little Vintage White.

2. Double load a 3/4-inch (19mm) flat with Hauser Green Light and Thicket. Keeping the Hauser Green Light to the outside, paint large, ruffled-edge leaves. Watch the outer edge to make sure you are ruffling the leaves with the movement of your brush.

3. Repeat the second half of the leaf using the same movement. Slide to the tip to meet the first half and finish the leaf. Chisel in a stem from the main vine halfway up to the tip of the leaf.

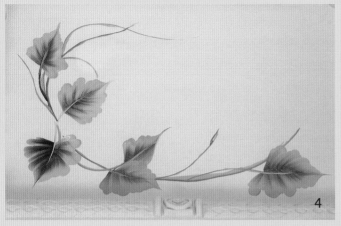

4. Paint the rest of the large leaves with the same brush and colors, following the growth direction of the vines. Attach the leaves with stems pulled halfway into the centers of the leaves.

5. Using the dirty brush (see "Tip") with a lot of floating medium, add a variety of shadow leaves to fill in.

6. Load a no. 16 flat with Inca Gold Metallic and a touch of Yellow Ochre and paint the ribbon (see page 23).

7. Double load a no. 10 filbert (see page 15) with School Bus Yellow and Yellow Ochre. Begin painting the comma-stroke flower petals that make up the chrysanthemums (see page 20 for step-by-step instructions on painting comma strokes).

Tip A "dirty brush" is usually the last brush you were using. Do not rinse it out—it should still have paint in it.

8. Using the same brush, stroke and colors, add the second layer of petals below the first. This layer should be wider than the first one to create the look of roundness.

9. Add the bottom layer of petals using School Bus Yellow, Yellow Ochre, with a touch of True Burgundy. Alternate picking up each color; the color on the top of the bristles when you are stroking is the one that shows up when you stroke. Allow some of these lower petals to droop here and there.

10. Finish painting the mums, continuing to alternate back and forth between the colors. Vary the sizes of the blossoms for a more interesting design. Here I have placed the largest mums in the lower corner, and smaller ones as they get closer to the ends of the vine. Double load a no. 16 flat with Hauser Green Light and Thicket and use the chisel edge to pull in the stems connecting the mums to the vine. Some stems will look as if they are in front of flowers and some will look as if they are behind flowers.

11. Double load a no. 12 flat with Hauser Green Light and Thicket. To paint the long, thin one-stroke leaves, begin on the chisel edge.

12. Push down on the bristles to form the widest part of the leaf.

13. Then slide and lift back up to the chisel to form the tip of the leaf.

14. Use a no. 2 script liner with inky Thicket to add some small comma-stroke leaves with a touch-and-pull motion; also add some curlicues. Still using your no. 2 script liner and inky Thicket, outline the leaves to give them dimension. Also add an extra line to accent the edge of some of the leaves.

15. This is a good time to step back and look at your design. You may find that you need to fill in an area with small leaves or curlicues. Use Inca Gold Metallic and your no. 2 script liner to embellish any areas that you want.

16. Load a no. 12 flat with Yellow Ochre and paint the raised designs on the frame of the tray. Accent with borders of True Burgundy.

17. After all paint has been allowed to dry completely, you may want to antique your tray to give it that heirloom look. Use a large flat brush to apply brown antiquing polish a section at a time.

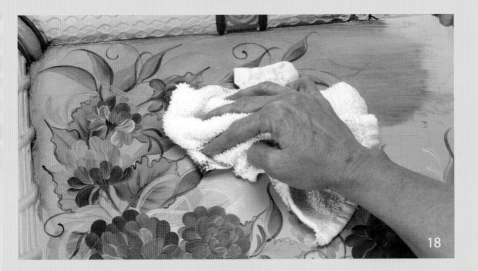

18

19

18. Before the antiquing polish dries, use a clean, soft cloth to rub off the excess polish and soften and blend the edges. (Always use a white cloth, as colored cloths may transfer some of their own color to the surface.)

19. Don't forget to use the antiquing polish on the frame of the tray also. Allow to dry thoroughly before using the tray.

Pumpkin & Cream Cheese Roll

CAKE MIXTURE
1 tsp. (5 ml) baking powder
1 8 oz. (227 gm) package cream cheese
2 tsp. (10 ml) cinnamon
1 tsp. (5 ml) pumpkin pie spice
1/2 tsp. (2.5 ml) ground nutmeg
1/2 tsp. (2.5 ml) salt
3 eggs slightly beaten
1 cup (237 ml) sugar
2/3 cup (158 ml) solid pack pumpkin

FILLING
1 cup (237 ml) confectioner's sugar
3/4 cup (177 ml) flour
6 tbsp. (89 ml) butter
1 tsp. (5 ml) vanilla
1 cup (237 ml) pecans

1. Preheat oven to 375°F (190°C). Grease a large jelly roll pan and then line with wax paper.
2. Combine flour, baking powder, cinnamon, pumpkin pie spice, nutmeg and salt in medium bowl, set aside.
3. In large bowl, beat eggs and sugar until fluffy, add pumpkin and mix well. Stir in dry ingredients all at once. Beat well, pour into wax paper-lined pan and spread evenly. Bake at 375°F (190°C) for 15 min.
4. Loosen cake around edges with knife if needed, then invert onto clean kitchen towel (cotton is best) that has been sprinkled heavily with confectioner's sugar. Roll cake up beginning at the short end. Place cake seam side down to cool.
5. For the filling, in a small bowl beat room-temperature cream cheese and butter until blended. Add vanilla and confectioners sugar, beat until smooth. Stir in the pecans.
6. Unroll cake and spread with filling, re-roll and refrigerate until ready to serve.

FolkArt Enamels Paints
- Wicker White
- Metallic Sterling Silver

One Stroke Glass/ Ceramics Brushes
- no. 2 script liner

Surfaces
- Blue glass plates, mugs and bowls are available at department stores, craft supply stores and discount stores.

warm winter's night

This last Christmas my youngest daughter Anna gave me a card that had glittery snowflakes on the front. Since we live in Florida, snow is not something we see unless we travel north. With Anna's card to inspire me, I decided that a cobalt blue glass mug was the perfect surface on which to paint fun and simple snowflakes—and a wonderful way to bring snow to Florida!

You can paint a complete table setting with snowflakes, including plates, bowls, place cards and centerpieces. Paint some snowflakes on dark blue cardstock and cut them out, attach them to thin sticks or wire and insert them into the centerpieces. Make several of them and attach to a string to create a garland for decorating a hutch, wall or window.

Add the glow of candlelight and you have the makings of a warm and snuggly winter's night.

FolkArt Enamels Colors

Wicker White   Metallic Sterling Silver

A Warm Treat for the Kids

Surprise the kids after a day of sled-riding or snowman-building. Fill snowflake-painted mugs with hot cocoa topped with lots of marshmallows!

If you don't live in an area where it snows during the holidays, gather the kids together for a favorite "holiday movie" night (be sure to choose a movie with lots of snow). Fill a painted glass bowl with snowy white popcorn, and add a colorful candy cane to a mug of hot cocoa in celebration of winter.

1. Begin painting the snowflake with long crossed lines, using a no. 2 script liner with inky Wicker White.

2. Connect the crossed lines in the center with short curved lines. Then add more long lines in between from the connecting lines. Begin pulling tendrils from the ends of the lines.

3. Use the handle end of the brush to dot in the center dot with Metallic Sterling Silver. Finish the snowflake with small and large Wicker White dots at the ends of every line.

4. Load a no. 2 script liner with inky Metallic Sterling Silver. Begin painting the silver scroll-work with a comma stroke.

5. Pull another stroke around and down on each side of the first comma stroke.

6. Continue adding curving strokes to make as many silver scrolls as you want. Let dry.

7. Each mug you paint will be as unique as every snowflake.

Use Your Imagination

What you paint is limited only by your imagination. So surprise yourself and your friends and paint a whole set of dishes inspired by the beauty of snowflakes. Just remember to keep the paint on the outsides of any mugs, bowls or drinking glasses, and place a clear glass plate over your painted plates for serving food.

brighten the
holidays

Paint the holidays brighter! Take the ordinary and make it extraordinary with a touch of paint and your imagination. A beautiful set of china can become unique by painting holiday greenery accented with ribbons and berries. A cookie jar becomes more than just a cookie jar when painted with gingerbread kids and a decorated tree. Make every ornament sparkle by embellishing with seasonal colors, metallic paint and crystals. And don't forget to paint a special jack-o'-lantern for your favorite trick or treaters!

FolkArt Enamels Paints
- Wicker White
- Metallic Sterling Silver
- Inca Gold Metallic
- Fresh Foliage
- Thicket

One Stroke Glass/Ceramics Brushes
- no. 6 flat
- no. 8 flat
- no. 10 flat
- no. 12 flat
- no. 2 script liner

Supplies
- Clear Medium

Surfaces
- White china plates, cups and saucers from Olympic Enterprises, Inc. www.olympicdecals.com 330-746-2726. Plain white china table settings are available at craft stores, discount stores and department stores.

christmas eve party

Decorating with paint for the holidays will always be one of my favorite things to do. The colors can be vibrant and rich with reds and greens or richly elegant with gold and silver. Each year, wonderful new colors come out for us to enjoy.

This table setting project was inspired by the ribbons and decorations often used on gift packages. The embellishments are so pretty that I always save them to be used on future gift packages.

Something that my family likes to do each year at our Christmas party is to write our yearly goals or wishes on the backs of our placecards. We have a special gold box in which each person places their card to save and open the next Christmas.

Family traditions like these are made even more special with beautiful table settings you've created yourself.

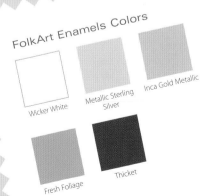

FolkArt Enamels Colors

Wicker White

Metallic Sterling Silver

Inca Gold Metallic

Fresh Foliage

Thicket

1. Dip the handle of your brush into a little paint and begin by dividing and marking the rim of the plate into three sections (or any odd number of sections that you want). Double load a no. 12 flat with Thicket and Fresh Foliage. Keeping the Fresh Foliage to the inside, paint the first side of the large leaves by wiggling out. Paint the second, smooth side of the leaves with a touch, push, slide and lift to the tip. Add a set of leaves to each section.

2. Load a no. 8 flat with Thicket and paint the little green leaves. These are tiny one-stroke leaves. You may need to pick up a small amount of clear medium (don't make the leaves too transparent).

3. Double load a no. 10 flat with Metallic Sterling Silver and Wicker White. Leading with the Wicker White, use the chisel edge of your bristles to touch-and-pull a set of silver blossoms in each section. For gold-colored blossoms, double load Inca Gold Metallic and Wicker White. Leading with the white, touch and pull each petal.

4. Load a no. 6 flat with Inca Gold Metallic to paint gold ribbons between each set (see page 23 for ribbon-painting techniques). The ribbon should go from wide to thin. Begin the ribbon on the chisel edge, then press down.

5. Lift back up to the chisel edge for the thin part of the ribbon.

6. Then lay the bristles down the other way for the wide part.

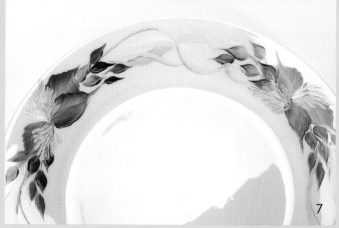

7

8

7. For the silver ribbons, load a no. 10 flat with Metallic Sterling Silver. Paint these ribbons in the same way, but intertwine them with the gold ribbons.

8. Add some gold one-stroke leaves here and there using the no. 10 flat and Inca Gold Metallic. Alternate Inca Gold Metallic and Metallic Sterling Silver on the end of your brush handle to dot silver and gold berries throughout.

Tip Paint the smaller dessert plates and the cups and saucers with a simpler design of silver and gold ribbons and small one-stroke leaves, using a mixture of the two greens used for the dinner plates (see the photo on page 52). This creates a complete table setting and looks especially elegant with your crystal stemware and good silver!

FolkArt Enamels Paints

- Engine Red
- Yellow Ochre
- Evergreen
- Hauser Green Medium
- Fresh Foliage
- Lemon Custard
- Wicker White
- Maple Syrup
- Licorice

One Stroke Glass/ Ceramics Brushes

- 3/4-inch (19mm) flat
- no. 6 flat
- no. 16 flat
- no. 12 flat
- small scruffy
- no. 2 script liner

Supplies

- Enamels Tip-Pen Set
- Flow Medium

Surface

- White ceramic cookie jars and bowls available at most department, discount and home stores.

holiday cookie jar

Many people make cookies for the holidays every year and give them away as gifts. This year start giving cookies in an extraordinary way! How about painting cookies on a container and then filling the container with the dry ingredients to make the cookies? Wouldn't that be fun! It is a lot faster than baking the cookies and decorating each one. Just be sure to include the how-to instructions for mixing and baking the cookies.

Another great holiday entertaining idea is this matching cookie jar and popcorn bowl project. They're easy and fun to make. Why not let the kids paint the cute faces on the gingerbread kids? It's a great way to include them in the decorating and they'll look forward to seeing their artwork every year at holiday time.

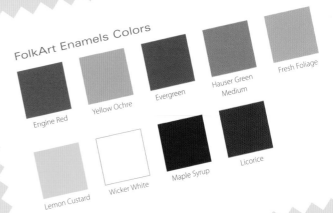

FolkArt Enamels Colors

Engine Red — Yellow Ochre — Evergreen — Hauser Green Medium — Fresh Foliage

Lemon Custard — Wicker White — Maple Syrup — Licorice

1. Load a 3/4-inch (19mm) flat with Engine Red and paint the bottom edge and the lid handle of the cookie jar. (You'll add the striping to the lid handle later.) Paint the Christmas tree using the chisel edge of a no. 16 flat, alternating between Evergreen, Fresh Foliage and Hauser Green Medium.

2. Load a no. 12 flat with Lemon Custard; sideload with Yellow Ochre and add the star at the top of the tree.

3. Basecoat the gingerbread kids using a no. 12 flat double loaded with Yellow Ochre and Maple Syrup. Keep the Maple Syrup to the outside to create roundness and depth to the gingerbread kids.

4. Use a small scruffy double loaded with Hauser Green Medium and Wicker White to pounce the garland on the tree.

5. Use the same technique with Wicker White and a touch of Engine Red to pounce the pink cheeks on the gingerbread kids' faces. Work flow medium and Wicker White into a 3/4-inch (19mm) flat and add white stripes to the bottom edge of the jar.

6. Load a no. 2 script liner with Licorice to paint the faces and raisin buttons on the gingerbread kids. Or use the brush handle to dot on the eyes and buttons. The buttons on the tummy shouldn't be perfectly round because they're supposed to look like raisins.

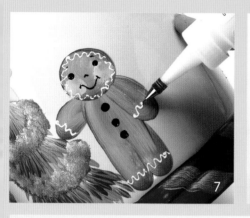

7

8

9

7. Place a metal Tip-Pen tip on the bottle of Wicker White and draw wavy icing lines on the gingerbread kids.

8. Also add white to the star on top of the tree, embellish the white stripes on the bottom edge of the jar, and dot a highlight in each eye. Use the brush handle of a no. 2 script liner to add white dots on the tree garland. Paint green stripes on the bottom edge of the jar using the script liner loaded with Evergreen and Fresh Foliage.

9. Using a no. 2 script liner with Engine Red, paint the bowtie and ribbons on the gingerbread kids. Use the brush handle to dot Engine Red onto the tree garland, then yellow dots with Lemon Custard.

    Paint the top edge of the cookie jar with Engine Red. Add candy cane stripes on the lid handle using straight Wicker White and a no. 6 flat. Begin at the bottom and turn your brush as you lift to the chisel. Use a no. 2 script liner with Fresh Foliage to add the green stripes.

Gumdrop Cookies

1/2 cup (118 ml) shortening
1 cup (237 ml) flour
1/2 cup (118 ml) brown sugar
1/2 tsp. (2.5 ml) baking soda
1/2 cup (118 ml) white sugar
1/2 tsp. (2.5 ml) baking powder
1 tsp. (5 ml) vanilla
1/4 tsp. (1.2 ml) salt
1 egg
1/2 cup (118 ml) diced gumdrops
1 cup (237 ml) quick oats

Cream shortening and sugar; add vanilla. Sift dry ingredients. Toss in gumdrops. Add oats with 1/4 cup (59 ml) of the flour mixture. Beat remaining flour in creamed mixture with beaten egg. Stir candy and oats in. Pinch off small pieces and roll into 1 inch (25 mm) balls. Flatten with spatula dipped in milk. Bake for about 10 minutes at 350°F (175°C). Makes about 5-1/2 dozen cookies.

To: Sarah

From: Jennifer

FolkArt Enamels Paints

- Inca Gold Metallic
- Pearl White Metallic
- Thicket
- Fresh Foliage
- Wicker White
- Engine Red

One Stroke Glass/ Ceramics Brushes

- 3/4-inch flat (19mm)
- nos. 2, 6, 8 and 12 flats
- no. 2 script liner

Supplies

- Kandi Kane Applicator Wand and rhinestones: www.KandiCorp.com
- Swarovski crystals
- craft tweezers
- Tip-Pen Set
- Paint Eraser tool (chisel)

Surfaces

- Donna Dewberry designed the four flat china ornaments for Mr. and Mrs. of Dallas: www.Dallaschina.com
- Glass ball ornaments

christmas ornaments

Every Christmas I have a tradition that I love. I paint an ornament for each of my children and grandchildren. They look forward to receiving such a special gift made with love.

Start your own Christmas tradition by painting the elegant ornaments in this project. You could also paint some for your own tree or to give as gifts for your friends and loved ones.

How about adding extra sparkle to your tree by enhancing the ornaments with rhinestones? You'll learn two different methods of attaching rhinestones to ornaments—using paint, or a special tool made just for attaching rhinestones with hot glue.

You and your loved ones will cherish these beautiful, classic designs. So let's get started!

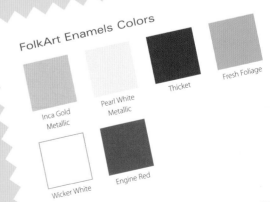

FolkArt Enamels Colors

Inca Gold Metallic

Pearl White Metallic

Thicket

Fresh Foliage

Wicker White

Engine Red

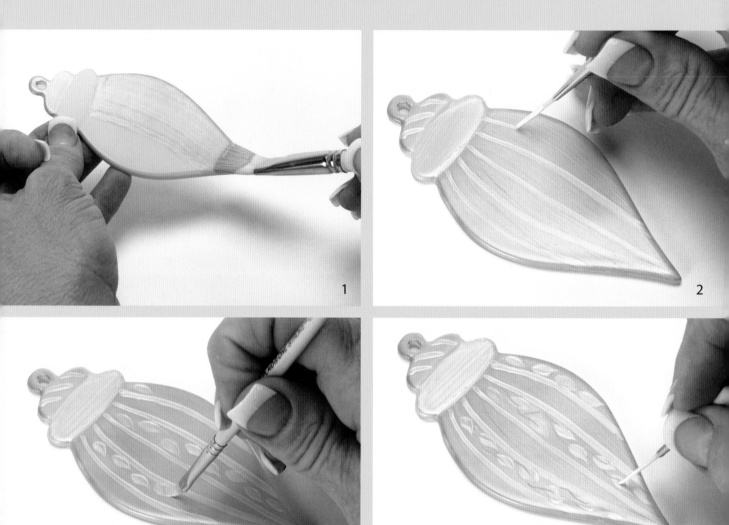

Gold-and-White Striped Ornament

1. Basecoat the drop part of the white china ornament with Inca Gold Metallic and a 3/4-inch (19mm) flat brush. Make sure to use long, smooth strokes, not short, choppy ones. Also, using a larger brush creates a smoother stroke on ceramics. Basecoat the top section with Pearl White Metallic.

2. Load a no. 2 script liner with Pearl White Metallic. Add little diagonal stripes around the hanger portion. With the same brush and

color, paint the stripes following the shape of the ornament. Keep them evenly spaced.

3. Load a no. 12 flat with Pearl White Metallic and paint tiny one-stroke leaves in every other stripe.

4. Add tiny vines between the leaves using a no. 2 script liner and Pearl White Metallic.

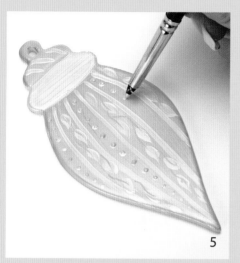

5

6

7

5. Add a line of evenly-spaced Pearl White Metallic dots to the other stripes using the Paint Eraser tool with the chisel point.

6. Add dots of white paint around the top section, then drop on some clear crystals using craft tweezers.

7. Your finished ornament will look similar to this one, but feel free to take elements from my design to create an ornament of your own design. Try this idea on ornaments of different shapes, too.

Extra-Special Gifts

For those one-of-a-kind gifts for special people in your life, try adding one of your handpainted ornaments to the gift wrapping. Just tie it on with a pretty coordinating ribbon; it really dresses up the giftwrap and it becomes a second gift! If your gift is going to be shipped or mailed, or if it might be mishandled, paint the ornament on a wooden or metal cutout instead of ceramic or glass. They come in all shapes and sizes and can be found at craft supply stores during the fall and winter months.

White Berries and Leaves

1. Basecoat a teardrop-shaped ornament with Pearl White Metallic using a 3/4-inch (19mm) flat. Load a no. 2 script liner with Inca Gold Metallic and add crosshatching around the top section. Sideload a 3/4-inch (19mm) flat and add a horizontal band of Inca Gold Metallic, following the shape of the ornament. Stroke across the ornament for the top edge of the band, flip the brush over, and stroke back across the ornament for the bottom edge of the band. Double load a no. 8 flat with Fresh Foliage and Thicket and stroke in the leaves.

2. Add the little white berries using the handle of your brush and Pearl White Metallic. Load a no. 2 script liner and dot the blossom ends on the berries with Thicket.

3. Embellish with two rows of clear gemstones just above and below the gold band. Apply evenly spaced dots of white paint, then use tweezers to set each gemstone in the paint dots (see Step 6 on page 63). Let dry.

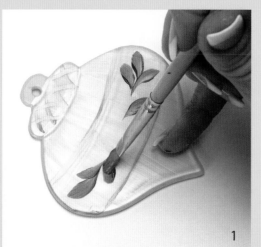

1

2

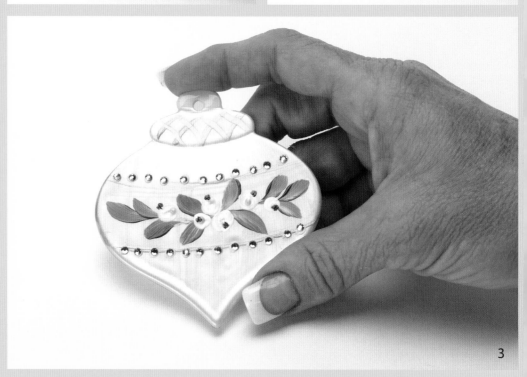

3

Holly Leaves and Pine Needles

1. Paint the top hanger section of the ornament with Pearl White Metallic on a no. 8 flat. Load a no. 8 flat with Fresh Foliage and sideload into Thicket. Paint the holly leaves, then stroke on the pine needles with the chisel edge of the brush (see page 21 for step-by-step instructions on painting holly leaves and pine needles).

2. Load a no. 2 script liner with Thicket and pull in some dark green stems for the red rhinestone holly berries.

3. Use Wicker White with a metal Tip Pen to add the white snow on the pine needles and to paint the wavy border around the edge of the ornament. To apply the red holly berries, use the brush handle end of a no. 2 script liner to dot Engine Red paint onto the ornament along the dark green stems. Use craft tweezers to drop a red rhinestone onto each dot of red paint. Let dry.

Holiday Cheese Ball

2 8-oz. pkgs. (454 g) cream cheese
1 cup (237 ml) crushed pineapple,
    well drained
2 cups (474 ml) chopped pecans
    (save 1/2 cup (118 ml) to cover
    the outside of the ball)
1/4 cup (59 ml) chopped green
    pepper
1 Tbsp. (15 ml) Everglades seasoning
    (optional)
Dash hot pepper sauce (optional)
Parsley

Mix and roll into a log or form into a
ball. Cover with chopped pecans and
decorate with strips of green and red
pepper and parsley. Cover and chill
overnight. Great holiday appetizer.

1

2

3

4

Pine Boughs and Ribbons

1. Load a no. 6 flat with Pearl White Metallic. Paint the white stripes by pressing down on the flat of the brush. Add green ribbons with Fresh Foliage and little Thicket on a no. 2 flat.

2. Chisel in the pine boughs using a no. 6 flat with Fresh Foliage and a touch of Thicket.

3. Attach a metal Tip-Pen tip on the Wicker White and draw wavy lines on the white stripes.

4. Dot Engine Red on the pine boughs and drop on red rhinestones using tweezers. Let dry.

Applying Rhinestones with an Applicator Wand

1. Another way to apply rhinestones, gemstones, pearls, beads and crystals to your ornaments is by using a specially designed applicator wand. It comes with several sizes of metal heads. Use the wand to pick up each pre-glued rhinestone or crystal. The heat from the applicator wand heats the glue.

2. Lightly touch the glue-side of the crystal to the ornament. It takes only a few seconds for the glue to cool and set. If you're using crystals that are not pre-glued, use a hot glue gun to apply a small dot of glue to the ornament, then set your crystal on the dot of glue. Let dry.

pumpkin fun!

FolkArt Outdoor Paints
- Pure Orange
- School Bus Yellow
- Green Forest
- Violet Pansy
- Maple Syrup
- Grass Green
- Yellow Ochre
- Licorice
- Wicker White
- Sunflower

FolkArt Outdoor Dimensional Paints
- Fresh Foliage
- Licorice

Brushes
- 3/4-inch (19mm) flat
- nos. 12 and 16 flats
- no. 2 script liner
- Large and small scruffy

Supplies
- Clear Medium
- Flow Medium

Surfaces
- Papier-mâché pumpkins available at craft stores

I always look forward to Halloween and the beginning of the fall holidays; the weather is changing, the leaves are turning and the season of festivity is nearing.

Let's delight our ghoulish guests this holiday season by decorating with these funny-face painted pumpkins. You can paint on a multitude of pumpkin-shaped surfaces such as papier-mâché, plastic or best of all—a real pumpkin! Stores that sell craft supplies or closeout merchandise are great places to find pumpkins made of a fibrous papier-mâché type material. Unlike real pumpkins, these can be stored and used year after year. They are lightweight and come already painted orange.

FolkArt Outdoor Colors

Pure Orange · School Bus Yellow · Green Forest · Violet Pansy · Maple Syrup · Grass Green

Outdoor Dimensional

Yellow Ochre · Licorice · Wicker White · Sunflower · Fresh Foliage · Licorice

Painting on Gourds

Dried gourds are also fun to paint on and come in all shapes and sizes. You'll find them at harvest bazaars and county fairs, or at the craft supply stores during the fall season.

One idea that's great fun is to turn a large gourd upside-down and paint a scarecrow face on it. Then stuff a jacket and pants with straw and place the "head" in the collar.

Another idea you might want to try is to create a Thanksgiving centerpiece by painting a turkey on a gourd. Gourds can grow in many odd shapes, so look for one that resembles the shape of a turkey with a big bulbous body and a curving neck. The funnier, the better!

Outdoor Colors:
Pure Orange
Licorice
School Bus Yellow
Grass Green
Wicker White
Yellow Ochre
Maple Syrup

Outdoor Dimensional Colors:
Fresh Foliage

Jack-o'-Lantern

1. If your pumpkin isn't already painted orange, basecoat it with Pure Orange Outdoor Paint (except for the stem). Sketch a jack-o'-lantern face onto your pumpkin. With a no. 2 script liner and inky Licorice, outline the face. Paint a line around the top to define the lid. Fill in the eyes and nose with Licorice.

2. Paint a variety of leaves on the top, using a 3/4-inch (19mm) flat double loaded with School Bus Yellow and Grass Green. Wiggle the brush down to the tip of the leaf, keeping the School Bus Yellow to the outside edge.

3. Paint the second side of the leaf in the same manner, wiggling down to the tip. The leaves should radiate outward from the pumpkin's stem.

4. Pull chisel-edge stems into the leaves, leading with the Grass Green side of the brush.

5. Load a no. 2 script liner with inky Wicker White and accent the face and lid lines.

6. Load a no. 12 flat with clear medium and sideload into School Bus Yellow. Float yellow highlighting on the left side of each eye, under the mouth and on the cheeks.

7. Add the eyeballs using a no. 12 flat with Wicker White and a little School Bus Yellow; these are simple C-shaped strokes.

8. Double load a no. 12 flat with Yellow Ochre and Maple Syrup. Use the chisel edge of the brush to paint in the straw around the top under the lid line. Paint the straw in clumps, not evenly.

9. Outline the leaves using Fresh Foliage dimensional paint straight from the bottle, using the tip to draw with. Add a few tendrils and curlicues here and there.

10. Using Outdoor paint lets you safely display your pumpkin on your front porch; the weather won't hurt the paint once it's dry.

1

2

3

4

Outdoor Colors:

Wicker White
Yellow Ochre
Pure Orange
Maple Syrup
Licorice
Green Forest
Sunflower

Candy Corn Faces:

1. Draw the candy corn shapes onto the pumpkin. Use a 3/4-inch (19mm) flat to basecoat the three colors of the candy corn. Use Wicker White for the top section, Yellow Ochre for the center area and Pure Orange for the bottom.

2. Load a no. 12 flat with clear medium and sideload into Maple Syrup. Float shading as shown to define the three areas.

3. Load a no. 2 script liner with Licorice to paint the faces. Use the end of your brush handle with Wicker White to add the polka dots on the bottom section. Also dot in a touch of Wicker White to highlight the eyes.

4. Paint leaves on the top radiating outward from the stem using a no. 16 flat double loaded with Green Forest and Sunflower. Finish with curlicues using a no. 2 script liner and inky Green Forest.

1

2

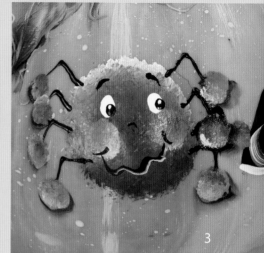

3

Outdoor Colors:

Wicker White
Violet Pansy
Grass Green
School Bus Yellow
Licorice

Outdoor Dimensional Colors:

Licorice

Silly Spider

1. For a different look, try basecoating part of your pumpkin with a ghoulish green color and add a friendly purple spider. The leaves around the top of the pumpkin's stem and the jack-o'-lantern face are painted as shown on pages 70-71. To paint the spider, double load a large scruffy with Violet Pansy and Wicker White and pounce on the body of the spider (keep the white to the top for roundness).

2. Use Licorice dimensional paint straight from the bottle to draw on the eight legs.

3. Double load a small scruffy with Grass Green and Wicker White and pounce on the spider's cheeks and feet. The eyes are Wicker White with Licorice details. Use a no. 2 script liner and Licorice to paint the eyebrows and mouth. Finish by adding the white highlights on the eyes and mouth using Wicker White and a no. 2 script liner.

Tip If you make a mistake, use one of your Paint Eraser tools to wipe the paint off before it dries.

special
occasions

We all enjoy celebrating the special occasions in our lives, sentimental times that are shared with our friends and family. With a little paint and enthusiasm, you can transform your next party and make it one to be remembered. When giving your next baby shower or birthday party, paint the chosen theme on the plates, napkins, cups, balloons, even the cake and snacks can be painted—nothing is off limits! You can create a sparkling table by embellishing an elegant set of china using simple comma strokes and metallic paints. Pair these with a beautiful table runner and napkins in coordinating colors, and you'll have a spectacular designer look to your dinner party!

CRIB
NOTES

FolkArt Papier Paints
- Wicker White
- School Bus Yellow
- Licorice
- Aqua
- Hot Pink
- Fresh Foliage
- Amethyst Metallic

One Stroke Brushes
- Small and large scruffy

One Stroke Brushes for Paper
- no. 16 flat
- no. 8 filbert

Supplies
- FolkArt One Stroke Adhesive Background Template: Squares

Surfaces
- Green paper plates, napkins and drink cups, and white gift bag with handles available at grocery stores, party supply stores, discount and craft supply stores.

baby shower

A theme makes throwing a party so much easier. When I'm planning a baby shower, I love to pick a special theme that relates to the mother and her future baby. I then coordinate the chosen theme by painting the invitations, cups, plates, even the napkins using FolkArt Papier opaque and dimensional paint. Interesting themes might include nature, teddy bears, Noah's ark, ABC's, under the sea, or themes using bold colors or pastels.

Most of all, keep it simple so you can finish the decorating with just a few quick steps, as I've done for you on the following pages.

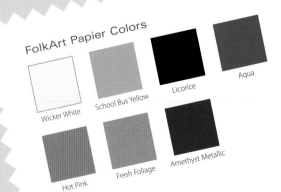

FolkArt Papier Colors

Wicker White   School Bus Yellow   Licorice   Aqua

Hot Pink   Fresh Foliage   Amethyst Metallic

Papier Paint Colors:
Wicker White
School Bus Yellow
Licorice
Aqua
Hot Pink

Papier Metallics:
Amethyst

Butterfly Plate

1. To paint the small green paper plates, double load a no. 16 flat with Wicker White and School Bus Yellow and stroke in the five-petal flowers (see page 24).

2. With the tip of the Wicker White bottle, double outline the flower—be really loose and informal with these lines.

3. With the tip of the Licorice bottle, add a black swirl for the flower center.

4. Begin the butterfly wings using a no. 16 flat double loaded with Aqua and Wicker White, keeping the white to the outside. (This stroke is the same as the heart-shaped leaf shown on page 18.)

5

6

7

8

5. Add the second set of wings using the same brush, colors and technique.

6. Double load a small scruffy with Amethyst Metallic and Wicker White and pounce on five segments for the head and body of the butterfly. Keep the white to the top.

7. Dab on the little butterfly cheeks using Hot Pink on a no. 8 fil-

bert, and highlight the eye with a dot of Wicker White. Use the Wicker White bottle tip to draw detail lines on the butterfly wings. Finish with Licorice antennae lines.

8. The large paper plates are painted in the same way; simply add two more flowers. The paper drink cups and napkins are stamped with a School Bus Yellow rectangle, then the same butterfly is painted. I drew lots of ruffly lines on the wings with Wicker White.

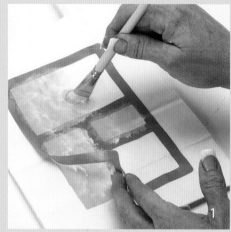

1

2

3

4

Papier Paint Colors:

Wicker White
School Bus Yellow
Hot Pink
Licorice
Aqua
Fresh Foliage

Papier Metallics:

Amethyst

Butterfly Gift Bag

1. Apply the adhesive background template to the front of the paper gift bag; press it down tight. Double load a large scruffy with Wicker White and School Bus Yellow and pounce on the color. Remove the template.

2. Double load a no. 16 flat with Hot Pink and Wicker White and paint the first layer of the flower, keeping the Hot Pink to the outside.

3. Add the second layer of petals using the same brush and colors. This layer's petals are shorter and fewer than the first.

4. Paint the flower stem and the leaves using a no. 16 flat double loaded with Fresh Foliage and Wicker White.

5. Paint the butterfly just like you did on the green paper plates (see pages 78-79). Add dimension to the butterfly and leaves using Wicker White straight from the bottle tip. Outline the flower petals with Hot Pink. Remember to keep it loose and fun!

6. Personalize the gift bag with a painted name tag! The five-petal flowers are Hot Pink and Wicker White. One flower has pink to the outside, the other two have white to the outside. Paint them, then cut out and glue them to the tag. Use Fresh Foliage to paint the flower center swirls and the name on the tag. Use Hot Pink to paint the border.

7. Tie on the name tag with a raffia bow.

Create A Lasting Memory

I love to create a scrapbooking page for the mom-to-be with photos and items from her baby shower. You can add some fabric from the table-cloth or paint the theme you paint-ed for the shower right on the page using Papier paints. Once the baby arrives, create a special scrapbook page on which mom can place a picture of her bundle of joy.

Another idea in place of shower games is to offer the guests lots of embellishments and glue and pass around an instant-shot camera, then have each person create their own page at the shower by adding their own sentiments to the page along with their photos. The mom-to-be would then have a whole scrapbook to someday share with her new baby!

happy birthday!

FolkArt Enamels Paints
- Evergreen
- Wicker White
- Licorice
- Butler Magenta
- Violet Pansy
- Cobalt
- Engine Red

One Stroke Glass/Ceramics Brushes
- 3/4-inch (19mm) scruffy
- nos. 2 and 12 flats
- no. 2 script liner

Supplies
- Clear Medium
- FolkArt One Stroke Adhesive Background Template: Circles or Dots
- AmeriColor Soft Gel Paste Food Color, available from Julie Motley (see Resources, page 158).

Surfaces
- White china plates are available at craft and home stores and department stores.

I love to go all out for birthday celebrations, including painting the dishes for the party. Balloons always add fun and color to a birthday celebration, so I'm sharing a fun little project that you can easily paint to brighten up any birthday celebration. You can paint the balloons any color to go along with your chosen color theme.

To make the party extra festive, get balloons that have been filled with helium and tie one to the back of each guest's chair with a length of curling ribbon. You can also tie a small sandbag weight onto several balloons and create a colorful balloon bouquet for the centerpiece. Sprinkle sparkly metallic confetti on the table and add ribbon streamers, and you have an unforgettable celebration!

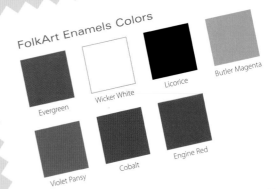

FolkArt Enamels Colors

Evergreen
Wicker White
Licorice
Butler Magenta
Violet Pansy
Cobalt
Engine Red

1

Million Dollar Cake

2 cups (474 ml) sugar
1/2 cup (118 ml) milk
2 sticks (227 g) butter
1 cup (237 ml) finely crushed nuts
6 eggs (one at a time)
1 cup (237 ml) flaked coconut
1 box vanilla wafers, finely crushed

Combine all ingredients, place in a
greased 9"x13" (23 cm x 33 cm) pan.
Bake 1 hour at 325°F (160°C).

Since this is a sheet-pan cake, it would
be easy to frost it with regular icing to
which you've added natural food col-
oring in the color of your choice. Or
buy white icing in a can, roll out a fondant, place it on the cake and paint a
design using AmeriColor Soft Gel
Paste Food Color (see Resources, page
158). Many bakeries will also make you
a fondant-covered cake to which you
can add your own design.

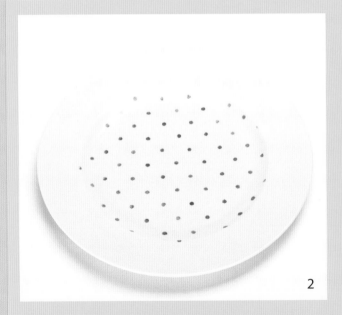

2

1. Use the adhesive back-
ground template with the
dots and apply the first set
of dots anywhere on plate.
Load a 3/4-inch (19mm)
scruffy and lightly pounce
on Evergreen. Remove the
template and reposition to
continue pouncing on the
Evergreen dots. You can
stagger the dots or you can
line them up in a pattern.

2. Depending on the shape
of your plate, you can
choose whether to apply
dots to the rim, or just keep
them in the center.

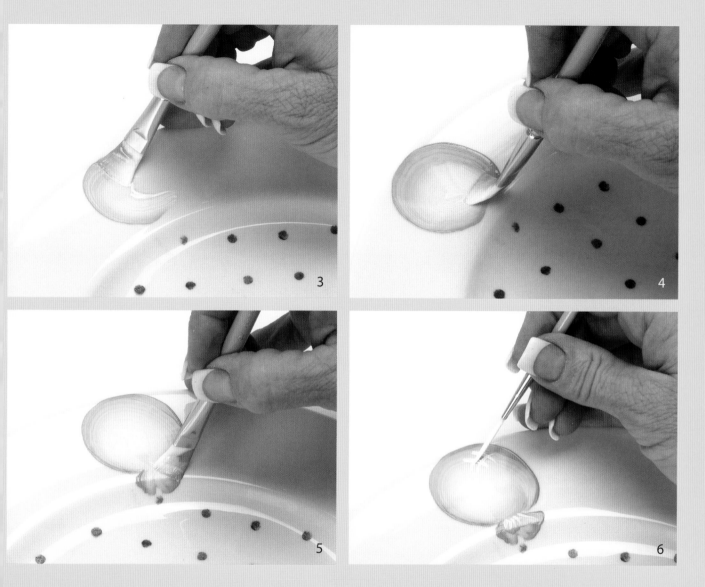

3. Double load a no. 12 flat with Wicker White and Butler Magenta and dip into clear medium. Paint the first half of the light-pink balloon in a half circle shape. Keep the pink to the outside. You might have to go over this a couple of times to smooth it out.

4. Paint the second half of the balloon in the same manner, still keeping the pink to the outside.

5. Paint the neck of the balloon using the same brush, wiggling in and out to create a gathered edge.

6. Load inky Wicker White on a no. 2 script liner and add highlights to the rounded part of the balloon and the neck gathers to show reflections.

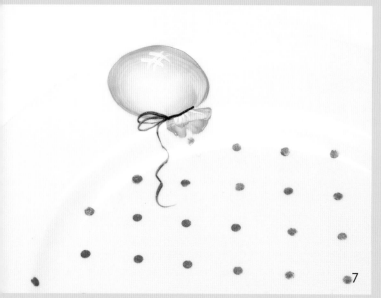

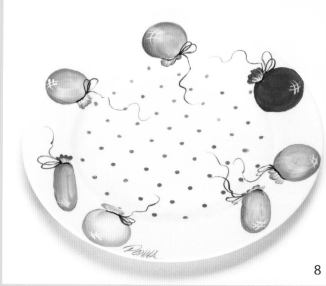

7. Load a no. 2 script liner with inky Licorice, and draw the string tie around the neck of the balloon.

8. Paint more balloons around the rim in a variety of shapes. The technique is the same as shown in Steps 3 through 7, even for the oblong balloons. Except for the Engine Red (see Tip, below), for each balloon double load a no. 12 flat with Wicker White and one other color: Butler Magenta, Violet Pansy, Cobalt or Evergreen. Always keep the darker color to the outside. Add reflective highlights with Wicker White on a no. 2 script liner, and finish with the string ties using Licorice.

9. Load a no. 2 flat with Engine Red and paint short, flat strokes for the confetti.

Tip Don't double load Engine Red with white or it will turn pink. Use a lot of clear medium and sideload the red on your brush (see page 15).

10. Add the confetti here and there in the empty spaces between the balloons and in the center. Turn your brush so your strokes are going in different directions.

11. Finish by using a no. 2 script liner and inky Cobalt (or your choice of color) to loosely paint some colorful curlicues. Let dry. If you want to use this project as a cake plate, place a clear glass plate between the cake and the painted plate.

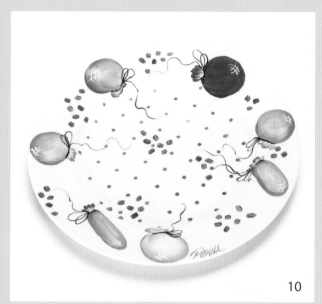

10

For a Special Treat

Painting cookies, cakes or cupcakes is easy and fun as well as a unique treat. I love to have the bakery prepare fondant-covered cookies or cakes. Or I buy white chocolate covered Oreos (shown above) and paint my theme onto them using AmeriColor Soft Gel Paste Food Color (see Resources, page 158). They're not only colorful and fun, they're also edible!

You can also pick up a can of white icing, roll out fondant and place it on your cake. Then use the Soft Gel Paste Food Color to paint your design on the birthday cake.

11

friends and neighbors

FolkArt Enamels Paints
- Wicker White
- Licorice
- Medium Gray

One Stroke Glass/ Ceramics Brushes
- 3/4-inch (19mm) scruffy
- no. 12 flat

Supplies
- FolkArt One Stroke Adhesive Background Template: Circles
- Paint Eraser tool

Surfaces
- Clear drinking glasses, pitchers and cake stands are available at craft supply stores, home stores and department stores.

When you have clear glass dishware, you can paint on the reverse side, which is the back or bottom of the plate or dish. With reverse painting, you must think ahead about what you want to see from the front.

I chose these particular colors because they can be used for any type of celebration, and they look great with my brightly colored table linens. Play upon this design using your own color choices. For a child's birthday celebration, use his or her favorite colors, or make it an anniversary setting by using gold, white, cream or silver. For a bridal shower, paint the pieces with the bride's wedding colors. The possibilities are endless.

This project is easy to paint, so don't try to make everything perfect. No two items will look alike—that's the fun of it all!

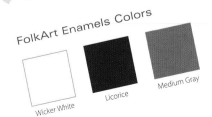

FolkArt Enamels Colors

Wicker White   Licorice   Medium Gray

1. Clean your glass piece with rubbing alcohol and a soft cloth to remove oils and fingerprints. Turn your cake stand upside down. You'll be reverse-painting on the underside of the plate. Apply the adhesive background template and, using the small circle, pounce on Licorice with a 3/4-inch (19mm) scruffy.

2. Apply the large circle template and pounce Wicker White using the 3/4-inch (19mm) scruffy. Allow the white circle to overlap the black one slightly.

3. Apply the medium-size circle on the template and pounce on

Medium Gray using the same scruffy. Continue pouncing on more circles, varying the sizes and colors to create an interesting design.

4. Turn the plate right side up to see how it looks from the front; adjust your design as needed. (Compare this view to step 3.)

5. Add wavy stripes of each color to the plate stand using a no. 12 flat. The stripes don't have to be perfect, just make them wavy.

6. Anytime you need to clean up the edges of your circles, use your Paint Eraser tool to carefully remove the excess paint.

7

8

9

10

7. The finished cake stand is a fun mixture of dots and stripes. And because the paint has been kept to the underside of the glass, you can set food directly on the top of the plate.

8. Use a no. 12 flat and paint wavy stripes of each color around the outside of some of the glasses.

9. Paint the outside of the other glasses with dots, varying the sizes and colors as you did

on the cake stand. Be sure the adhesive circle template is smoothed down to the glass so paint doesn't seep underneath.

10. Paint the outside of the glass pitcher with both stripes and dots to complete the set.

Enjoy the Day!
Any day can be a celebration when you have fun glassware that you painted yourself.

Invite a few special friends over and use your painted glassware to celebrate the day. Keep things simple, make your friends the center of attention. Set your table with a pretty tablecloth and napkins, serve cake and lemonade, and simply enjoy each other's company.

But be forewarned—your friends may want a painting lesson before they leave!

simply elegant

FolkArt Enamels Paints
- Inca Gold Metallic
- Wicker White

One Stroke Glass/ Ceramics Brushes
- 3/4-inch (19mm) flat
- no. 8 flat
- no. 2 script liner

Supplies
- Flow Medium

Surfaces
- White china table settings and accessories from Olympic Enterprises, Inc. www.olympicdecals.com 330-746-2726
- Plain white china table settings and accessories are available at craft supply stores, home stores, discount and department stores.

D on't wait for a reason to invite your friends and loved ones to your home, create one! Then make those times memorable and unique by setting your table with the look of elegant china. You can take the most inexpensive plain white dishes and make them look rich and stately with a few strokes of silver or gold paint. Only you know how easy it was to do!

In this project, I have used the same graceful comma-stroke design on a variety of dishes, crystal stemware and accessories. Then I arranged my dining table with color-coordinated linens and added a spark of color with a centerpiece of yellow roses. Even the simplest of foods look impressive and inviting in such a setting. And in the glow of evening candlelight, the gold and white colors of the china create a soft and romantic look for those dinners-for-two.

FolkArt Enamels Colors

Inca Gold Metallic

Wicker White

93

1. Clean the china surface with rubbing alcohol to remove oils and fingerprints. Take care not to touch the areas you are painting. Begin by brushing Inca Gold Metallic on the rim of the plate with a 3/4-inch (19mm) flat. If your plate has a textured design on the rim, drag the brush across the design and the textured area will catch the paint, creating a beautiful, dimensional effect.

2. Load a no. 8 flat with Wicker White and paint comma strokes in the center area. Begin on the chisel, apply pressure while pulling down, then slide back up to the chisel (see page 20).

3. Paint all the comma strokes that curve in toward each other.

4. Add the comma strokes that curve away, using the same technique and brush.

5. Now load a no. 2 script liner with Inca Gold Metallic. Paint smaller comma strokes and a few scrolls in among the white commas.

6. Turn the plate and repeat the design on the other half. Don't worry if the designs do not match exactly; this shows your plates are hand-painted, not mass-produced.

7

8

Use the same simple comma strokes, colors and brushes to paint cups, saucers, teapots, sugar and creamers and even crystal stemware to match your plates.

Keep it simple, and allow the shape of your china to dictate the amount of paint and the type of strokes you use. Trust your instincts; you'll be surprised how lovely a table setting you can create with a small amount of paint and your imagination.

With china and glassware as beautiful as these, I suggest you handwash them rather than putting them in the dishwasher. They may become heirlooms that will pass down through your family, so you'll want to take very good care of them.

Inspire your Guests

Consider how often you get to set a table with your best pieces. Don't save your prettiest china "for good." Take every opportunity to create a sparkling table setting with your painted dishes. I love to dress up my table with cut-crystal candlesticks with tall white candles (even if they're faux cut-crystal!). Lovely centerpieces can be created by simply varying the sizes and heights of the candlesticks and candles. Lay some baby's breath around the bottom of the candlesticks or add some fern leaves (keep this light and airy but full; not too sparse). Use the family silver to serve tea and cookies. Your guests will not only be impressed, they will also be inspired when you tell them how simple it is to create an elegant table.

dinnertime
with the family

Don't pass up an opportunity to celebrate the time
you spend with your family every day. Dinner around
the kitchen table can be as special as any occasion,
and any item that is used for ordinary meals can be
enhanced with a touch of paint. Brighten up a set of
casserole dishes with a blueberry theme. Take those
old, boring salt and pepper shakers off the shelf and
paint them with colorful and fun designs for gift giving
or for your own use. Revive a retro theme; if you have
an old tablecloth or kitchen towel that has seen better
days, bring it back to life with a 1940's design that you
carry over onto colorful dinner plates. With today's
modern paints and brushes, you can paint on fabrics
as easily as you paint on glass and ceramics.

blueberry casserole

FolkArt Enamels Paints
- Periwinkle
- Fresh Foliage
- Hydrangea
- Midnight
- Wicker White
- Thicket

One Stroke Glass/Ceramics Brushes
- no. 2 flat
- no. 8 flat
- no. 12 flat

Supplies
- Clear Medium

Surface
- White ceramic casserole dish with lid, available at home and department stores. White square tiles available at any home improvement center.

Create serving dishes that look beautiful right on your kitchen table! This lidded casserole dish painted with a fresh blueberry design is sure to go with almost any decorating style from blue-and-white traditional to a country look.

This set includes matching ramekins and would make a wonderful wedding or shower gift for that bride-to-be or a welcome-to-the-neighborhood gift for your new neighbor across the street.

The blueberries are surprisingly easy to paint with just two colors, and the tile trivets are fun to do with a freehand plaid design. I placed a color-coordinated hotpad under the casserole dish to complete the table setting. Time for dinner!

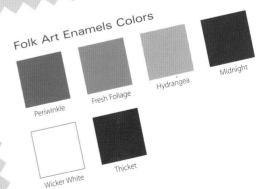

Folk Art Enamels Colors

Periwinkle   Fresh Foliage   Hydrangea   Midnight

Wicker White   Thicket

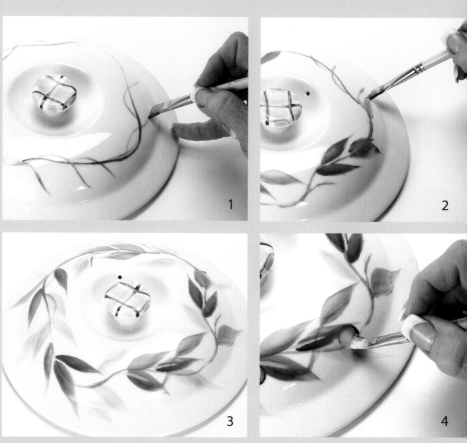

1. Clean the ceramic surface with rubbing alcohol to remove oils and fingerprints. Take care not to touch the areas you are painting. To paint the plaid design on the lid's handle, load a no. 8 flat with Hydrangea and, using the flat side of the brush, paint vertical stripes across the handle, then paint horizontal stripes. Load the same brush with Midnight and use the chisel edge to add thin vertical and horizontal stripes over the Hydrangea stripes. Double load a no. 12 flat with Fresh Foliage and Thicket and chisel in the vine around the lid. Now and then, add a touch of Periwinkle into the Thicket and Fresh Foliage.

2. Add chisel edge leaves (see page 19) using a no. 12 flat double loaded with Thicket and Fresh Foliage.

3. Use Clear Medium with Fresh Foliage to add some subtle, almost transparent shadow leaves.

4. To begin the blueberries, load a no. 8 flat with Hydrangea and sideload into Midnight. Paint a half circle, keeping the Midnight to the outside.

5

6

7

8

5. Flip the brush over and paint the other half of the berry, still keeping the Midnight to the outside. Paint each blueberry like this, one at a time, clustering them along the vine.

6. To paint the blossom end of each berry, load a no. 2 flat with Midnight, lay the brush flat and paint a little five-petal stroke. Paint the blossom end in a different place on each berry to make them look more natural.

7. Touch in a Wicker White highlight on each blossom end with one corner of a no. 2 flat. Let the paint dry completely.

8. Paint the blueberries, leaves and vine on the casserole dish and the ramekins using the same techniques as on the lid. The tile trivets are painted with the same plaid design as on the handle of the casserole lid (see step 1). Follow the paint manufacturer's instructions for baking and washing your finished pieces.

FolkArt Paints
• See following pages for colors for individual shakers

One Stroke Brushes
• nos. 2, 10, 16 flats

One Stroke Glass/ Ceramics Brushes
• nos. 2, 6, 8, 12 flats
• no. 2 script liner
• no. 6 filbert
• 3/4-inch (19mm) flat
• 3/4-inch (19mm) scruffy

One Stroke Brushes for Lettering
• no. 2 flat

Supplies
• FolkArt One-Stroke Adhesive Background Templates: Circles or Dots
• Enamels Detail Painters
• Flow Medium

Surfaces
• Salt and pepper shakers available at department stores, home stores and flea markets.

salt & pepper shakers

Collecting salt and pepper shakers is a fun and inexpensive hobby that many of us enjoy. I love to go to garage sales or antique shops searching for that perfect set to paint. You can also find them in home stores and the cookware sections in department stores.

Everyone can use salt and pepper shakers; they make delightful one-of-a-kind gifts for family or friends!

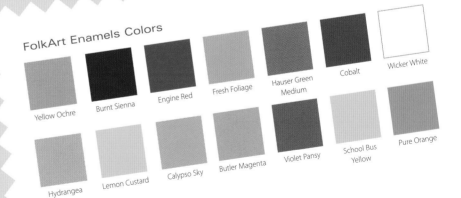

FolkArt Enamels Colors

Yellow Ochre · Burnt Sienna · Engine Red · Fresh Foliage · Hauser Green Medium · Cobalt · Wicker White

Hydrangea · Lemon Custard · Calypso Sky · Butler Magenta · Violet Pansy · School Bus Yellow · Pure Orange

FolkArt Outdoor Opaque Colors

Grass Green · Fresh Foliage · Burnt Sienna · Wicker White

1

2

3

4

5

6

FolkArt Enamels Paints:

Yellow Ochre

Burnt Sienna

Engine Red

Fresh Foliage

Hauser Green Medium

Cobalt

Wicker White

Country Morning Shaker Set — Rooster

1. Clean the shaker set with rubbing alcohol. Take care not to touch the areas you are painting. Double load Yellow Ochre and Burnt Sienna on a no. 8 flat brush for glass/ceramics, and paint three long comma strokes to define the body.

2. Using the same colors, continue to add more strokes for the wing and tail feathers.

3. Double load the no. 8 flat with Engine Red and Burnt Sienna and chisel in some brighter feathers.

4. Add some colorful green tail feathers using thick Fresh Foliage and Hauser Green Medium.

5. Paint the legs, feet and beak using Burnt Sienna and Yellow Ochre on a no. 2 script liner for glass/ceramics. Add the eye with the same brush and Cobalt.

6. Still using the no. 2 script liner and Cobalt, add a few blue tail feathers. Load the no. 8 flat with Engine Red and paint the comb and wattle.

7

8

9

10

Country Morning Shaker Set—Hen

7. Double load a no. 8 flat for glass/ceramics with Wicker White and Yellow Ochre and stroke in the head and body using long comma strokes.

8. Pick up more Wicker White on the same brush and add comma strokes to form the wing and tail feathers. Stroke in some light green feathers on the belly with Wicker White and Fresh Foliage.

9. Paint the legs, feet and beak using Yellow Ochre and Burnt Sienna on a no. 2 script liner. Add the eye with Cobalt. Load the no. 8 flat with Engine Red and paint the wattle and comb. Dot a Wicker White highlight in the eyes of both the rooster and hen.

10. Finish your salt and pepper shakers with a stripe around the top of each shaker using the no. 2 script liner with Engine Red. Follow the paint manufacturer's instructions for baking and washing your finished shakers.

FolkArt Enamels Paints:

Hydrangea
Lemon Custard
Wicker White

Polka Dot Shaker Set

1. Clean the shaker set with rubbing alcohol. Take care not to touch the areas you are painting. Apply the smallest circle part of the adhesive background template to the shaker's lid and pounce on Hydrangea with a 3/4-inch (19mm) scruffy brush for glass/ceramics.

2. Reapply the circle template to the glass part of the shaker and pounce more large circles with Hydrangea. Load a 5/8-inch (16mm) detail painter with Lemon Custard and dot on the medium-size circles.

3. Load a 1/4-inch (6mm) detail painter with Wicker White and dot on the smallest circles. Paint the second shaker, but don't try to make them look exactly alike. Follow the paint manufacturer's instructions for baking and washing your finished shakers.

1

2

3

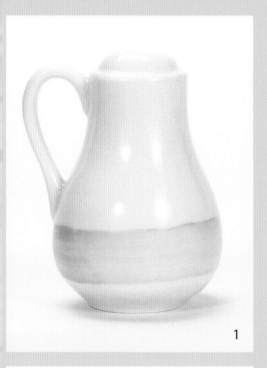

1

2

3

4

FolkArt Enamels Paints:

Calypso Sky
Butler Magenta
Wicker White
Fresh Foliage
Lemon Custard

Pastel Flower Shaker Set

1. Clean the shaker set with rubbing alcohol. Take care not to touch the areas you are painting. Use Flow Medium and Calypso Sky on a 3/4-inch (19mm) flat brush for glass/ceramics to paint a wide band around each shaker.

2. Double load a no. 8 flat for glass/ceramics with Butler Magenta and Wicker White and paint a six-petal flower over the top part of the blue band.

3. Double load the no. 8 flat with Fresh Foliage and Wicker White and paint the small one-stroke leaves. Use the handle end of your brush to add a dot of Lemon Custard in the center of the flower.

4. Finish with a narrow band of Calypso Sky around the top of each shaker using a no. 2 script liner. Follow the paint manufacturer's instructions for baking and washing your finished pieces.

1

2

3

4

5

6

FolkArt Enamels Paints:

Engine Red
Wicker White
Hauser Green Medium
Lemon Custard

Strawberry Shaker Set

1. Clean the shaker set with rubbing alcohol. Take care not to touch the areas you are painting. Double load a no. 8 flat brush for glass/ceramics with Engine Red and Wicker White and paint the left side of the strawberry using a C-shaped stroke. Pull in a little and back out to create the dimple at the bottom.

2. Flip the brush over and paint the right side of the strawberry, keeping the red to the outside.

3. Paint the small strawberry using the same brush, colors and strokes.

4. Double load a no. 2 flat with Hauser Green Medium and Wicker White and add some small one-stroke leaves and stems.

5. Use Hauser Green Medium on a no. 2 script liner to add curlicues. Pick up a little Lemon Custard on the same brush and touch on some seeds.

6. Finish by painting a small five-petal blossom using a no. 6 flat with Lemon Custard and a touch of Wicker White. Dot Hauser Green Medium stamens in the middle of the blossom. Follow the paint manufacturer's instructions for baking and washing your finished pieces.

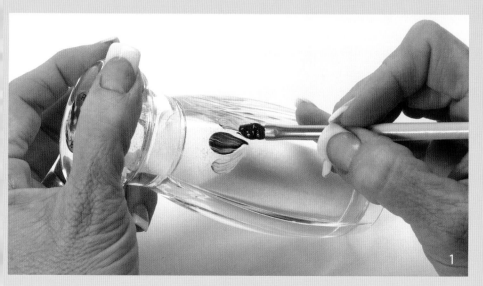

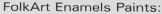

FolkArt Enamels Paints:

Violet Pansy
Wicker White
Lemon Custard
Hauser Green Medium

Iris Shakers

1. Clean the shaker set with rubbing alcohol. Take care not to touch the areas you are painting. Double load a no. 6 filbert brush for glass/ceramics with Violet Pansy and Wicker White. Paint the center petal of the tallest iris. Add more Wicker White to the brush and paint the two side petals with comma strokes.

2. Pick up a touch of Lemon Custard on the same brush and paint the bottom petals with comma strokes. Pick up a little more Lemon Custard and paint the center petal of the smaller iris. The two side petals are Violet Pansy comma strokes.

3. Pick up a tiny bit of Lemon Custard on the same brush and paint the two lower petals of the small iris. Dot a Lemon Custard center in the iris blossoms. Double load a no. 6 flat brush for glass/ceramics with Hauser Green Medium and Lemon Custard and chisel in the flower stems and the long pointed leaves. Follow the paint manufacturer's instructions for baking and washing your finished pieces.

FolkArt Outdoor Opaque Paints:
Grass Green
Fresh Foliage
Burnt Sienna
Wicker White

Letters and Checks Shaker Set

1. Load a no. 10 flat with Fresh Foliage and paint the light green band around the lower part of each shaker. Use a no. 16 flat with Grass Green and add some checks around the bottom. Just touch and pull short strokes, using the width of the brush as a measuring device for the spaces between the green checks. Add a Burnt Sienna band around the top using a no. 2 flat. Load a no. 2 flat brush for lettering with Burnt Sienna and freehand an "S" on the salt shaker and a "P" on the pepper mill.

2. Load a no. 2 flat with Burnt Sienna and use the chisel edge to paint stems. Using the same brush with Fresh Foliage and flow medium, paint little chisel-edge leaves. Place them over and around the lettering as shown.

3. Add a few clusters of tiny white blossoms using the chisel edge of a no. 2 flat and Wicker White.

1

2

3

1

2

1

2

FolkArt Enamels Paints:
School Bus Yellow
Pure Orange
Cobalt
Fresh Foliage

Colorful Stripes Shaker Set
1. Clean the shaker set with rubbing alcohol. Take care not to touch the areas you are painting. Paint a light green band around the lower part of the shaker using Fresh Foliage and a no. 2 flat. Add a wide band in the center using a 3/4-inch (19mm) flat with Pure Orange. Add a second wide band with School Bus Yellow.

2. Freehand some diagonal squares around the bottom with Cobalt on a no. 12 flat. Add a thin Cobalt line around the top using a no. 2 script liner. If you wish, reverse the orange and yellow center bands on the pepper mill so it will be different from the salt shaker. Follow the paint manufacturer's instructions for baking and washing your finished shakers.

FolkArt Enamels Paints:
Inca Gold Metallic
Wicker White

Simple and Elegant Shaker Set
1. Clean the shaker set with rubbing alcohol. Don't touch the areas you are painting. Use a no. 8 flat with Inca Gold Metallic to add vertical stripes on every other facet. If your shakers don't have facets, just space the stripes equally around. You may need a few coats to achieve the richness that you want (make sure each coat dries in between).

2. On the other facets, paint little one-stroke leaves with Wicker White on a no. 2 flat. Finish by adding gemstones to the leaves (see page 27). Follow the manufacturer's instructions for baking and washing your finished shakers.

111

FolkArt Enamels Paints

- Yellow Ochre
- Burnt Sienna
- Thicket
- Fresh Foliage
- Pure Orange
- Violet Pansy
- Burnt Umber

One Stroke Glass/Ceramics Brushes

- no. 16 flat

Surface

- Heavy ceramic crocks, canisters and bowls are available at any craft, department or home store.

tuscan kitchen

The classic look of old-world Italy is all about warm, muted colors that appear as if they have been around for a hundred years. It's easy to find large ceramic crocks and bowls that fit into a warm-toned color scheme. These make great fruit bowls and canisters for your kitchen counter. Paint your favorite fruit onto a crock using some of these Tuscany-inspired colors. You could even paint a border on your kitchen walls to match. Decorate with garlic braids and canisters filled with breadsticks or pasta, add a splash of tomato-red with curtains or table linens, and you'll feel like you're dining in an Italian villa.

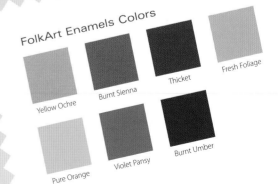

FolkArt Enamels Colors

Yellow Ochre   Burnt Sienna   Thicket   Fresh Foliage

Pure Orange   Violet Pansy   Burnt Umber

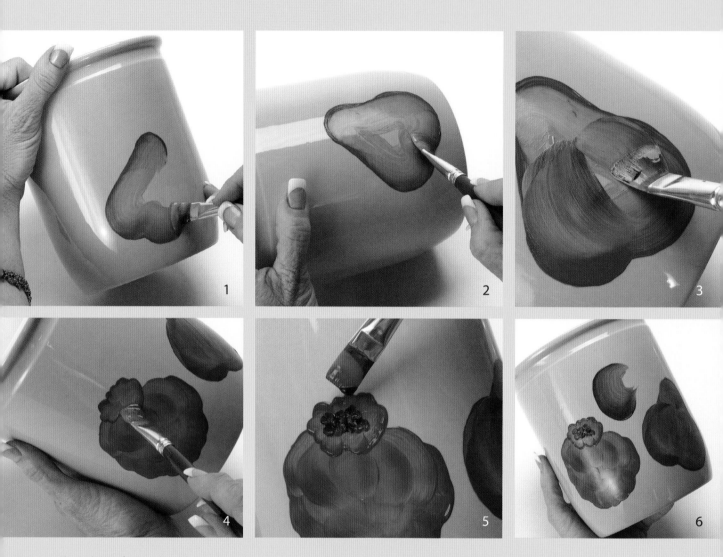

1. Clean the surface with rubbing alcohol. Don't touch the areas you are painting. Load Yellow Ochre on a no. 16 flat, sideload into Burnt Sienna, and begin the pear. Start at the top following the shape of the fruit; keep the Burnt Sienna to the outside.

2. Stroke in the second side of the pear, still following the shape of the fruit and keeping the Burnt Sienna to the outside.

3. Take the brush still loaded with Yellow Ochre and Burnt Sienna and double load a little Thicket and Fresh Foliage. Fill in the center of the pear with smooth curving strokes.

4. Double load a no. 16 flat with Pure Orange and Burnt Sienna and paint the pomegranate. Stroke this in following the shape of the fruit, keeping the Burnt Sienna to the outside. Paint the shape of the crown.

5. Dot in the center by dabbing on Thicket with the corner of your brush bristles.

6. With the orange still in your brush, pick up some Violet Pansy and stroke in the first side of the plum using a C-shaped stroke. Keep the Violet Pansy to the outside.

7. Add a teardrop-shaped stroke right on top of the first stroke to complete the plum.

8. Paint the second plum overlappping the first one using the same technique.

9. Load a no. 16 flat with Fresh Foliage, Thicket and a little Burnt Umber and fill in around the fruit with various leaves: chisel edge leaves, one-stroke and full leaves.

10. Load the same brush with Yellow Ochre and Violet Pansy and stroke in a few clusters of grapes along the bottom. It's okay to stroke over the leaves if they're wet. You may have to stroke over the green a couple of times to pick up the paint that is underneath.

Paint the large bowl with the same fruits, but space them out around the entire bowl (see page 112). Follow the paint manufacturer's instructions for baking and washing your finished pieces.

Entertain with Style

Add style to your kitchen with this set of beautiful painted crockery. These salad bowls are the same yellow as the bowl and crock in this project, but I've kept the design very simple: just a band of leaves and stems using Fresh Foliage and Thicket. These colors look great with a fresh green salad sparked with bright red tomatoes. Or fill them with healthy snacks for your family and drop-in guests, such as nuts, raisins or homemade granola bars.

Be creative with your glassware and table linens, too. Look for color-coordinated stemware and rustic textured napkins. An aged terra cotta pot of culinary herbs makes a beautifully natural centerpiece.

115

retro luncheon

FolkArt Acrylics and Enamels Paints
• See following pages for colors for individual items.

One Stroke Brushes
• 5/8-inch (16mm) angle

One Stroke Brushes for Paper
• no. 16 flat
• 5/8-inch (16mm) angle

One Stroke Glass/Ceramics Brushes
• nos. 12 and 16 flats
• no. 2 script liner

Surface
• White cotton tablecloths can be found at most department and home stores.
• Fiestaware table settings and accessories can be found at department or home stores as well as online. Original colors from the 1940s and 1950s can often be found at flea markets and antique stores.

I collect Fiestaware in bright, assorted colors. This painted table cloth and Fiestaware set is bright and fresh; a nostalgic look made new! Set your patio table with fresh, white linens; mix and match the colors of the Fiestaware, the brighter the better; then invite a group of friends over for an afternoon luncheon. The cheery colors of the painted dishes and tablecloth will make your luncheon one to be remembered. Don't forget to place clear glass plates over your painted plates for serving food.

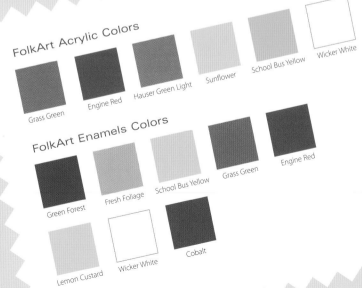

FolkArt Acrylic Colors

Grass Green · Engine Red · Hauser Green Light · Sunflower · School Bus Yellow · Wicker White

FolkArt Enamels Colors

Green Forest · Fresh Foliage · School Bus Yellow · Grass Green · Engine Red · Lemon Custard · Wicker White · Cobalt

1

2

FolkArt Acrylic Colors:

Grass Green
Engine Red
Hauser Green Light
Sunflower
School Bus Yellow
Wicker White
Cobalt
Green Forest

Table Cloth

1. Prewash and dry your white table cloth to remove any sizing. Don't use fabric softener in the rinse. To paint on fabric, you can use the One-stroke brushes for paper. Double load a no. 16 flat with Hauser Green Light and Wicker White. Stroke in the stems using the chisel edge. Paint the leaves using the same brush and colors, picking up a little Grass Green now and then.

2. Load a no. 16 flat with Engine Red and stroke in some large red blossoms and a few clusters of smaller buds. Fill in the large petals on the center flower.

3. Double load Sunflower and School Bus Yellow on a no. 16 flat and paint the petals on the yellow flowers. Sideload a little Wicker White to get some depth. With the same brush, load Engine Red and sideload into Green Forest; add some depth and shading to the petals of the red blossoms. With Hauser Green Light, highlight the small red buds.

3

4. Double load a no. 16 flat with Wicker White and Hauser Green Light and add centers to the large flowers. Pick up School Bus Yellow, Grass Green and some Wicker White here and there and stroke in some more leaves and stems. Load Cobalt on a 5/8-inch (16mm) angle brush and paint the blue flowers. Chisel in a few vines and leaves using the Cobalt.

5. Begin detailing the flowers, centers and leaves with the same colors you've been using; as you have each color on your brush, add the pin stripes around the corner if you are painting a square or rectangular cloth. Use Hauser Green Light with School Bus Yellow to fill in and highlight the smaller leaves. Shade the center of the large red blossom with Cobalt and the center of the yellow blossom with Engine Red. Detail some of the blue flowers with Engine Red, and others with Engine Red and Hauser Green Light.

4

5

FolkArt Enamels Paints:

Green Forest
Fresh Foliage
School Bus Yellow
Grass Green
Engine Red
Lemon Custard
Wicker White
Cobalt

Be sure to adjust the paint colors for each plate and the pitcher as needed so the colors show up well. For these plates and the pitcher, we will be using the Enamels Paints and the brushes for glass/ceramics.

Red plate:
1. Double load a no. 12 flat with Fresh Foliage and Grass Green and chisel in the stems. Use a no. 16 flat double loaded with School Bus Yellow and Lemon Custard to paint the large yellow flowers.

2. Paint the small five-petal flowers and the flower buds with Wicker White on a no. 12 flat.

3. Double load a no. 12 flat with Fresh Foliage and Grass Green and paint a variety of leaves.

4. The large flower center is Cobalt and shades of green and yellow. The small flower centers are red and yellow. With Cobalt, shade the white buds and finish with stems and leaves using a no. 2 script liner.

5

6

7

8

Yellow Pitcher:

5. Double load a no. 12 flat with Fresh Foliage and Grass Green and chisel in the stems and leaves. Use Engine Red on a no. 16 flat to paint the petals of the red flowers. Use Wicker White on a no. 16 flat to paint the white petal flowers. Touch in the flower centers using shades of red, green and yellow. Detail the red flowers and add some fernlike leaves using Cobalt and a no. 2 script liner.

Green plate:

6. Double load a no. 12 flat with Lemon Custard and Green Forest and chisel in the green stems. Use Engine Red on a no. 16 flat to paint the petals on the red flowers. Use Wicker White for the five-petal flowers. Load a no. 12 flat with Lemon Custard and add the small yellow flower petals. Still using your no. 12 flat, add some chisel-edge leaves with Fresh Foliage sideloaded with Lemon Custard, alternating with Green Forest. Paint some one-stroke leaves with Fresh Foliage. Add the flower centers using Cobalt and shades of red, green and yellow. Finally add some stems and small leaves using Cobalt and a no. 2 script liner.

Yellow Plate:

7. Follow the instructions for the yellow pitcher, adjusting the design to the size of the plate.

Blue Plate:

8. Follow the instructions for the red plate, adjusting the colors.

121

quick & easy
gift ideas

When you're searching for that unique gift idea you need quickly, look no further than the pages of this book. Gift giving has never been easier when you paint a simple design on a beautiful basket and fill it with gifts chosen from the heart. I'll also show you how to paint a bamboo design on a glass vase that's perfect for a man or woman. Try it, you'll be surprised how easily you can transform an ordinary vase into a gift that will be cherished.

FolkArt Outdoor Paints
- Magenta
- Violet Pansy
- Fresh Foliage
- Soft Apple
- Plum Vineyard
- Thicket
- Wicker White

One Stroke Brushes
- 1-inch (25mm) flat
- 3/4-inch (19mm) flat
- 2-inch (51mm) flat

Supplies
- FolkArt Enamels 5/8-inch (16mm) Detail Painter

Surface
- Basket with wooden lid and handle available from craft supply stores and home stores.
- Glass canning jars are available in cookware and grocery stores.

gift basket

Warm the heart of a new neighbor, school teacher, or a sick friend with a basket full of baked goods wrapped with care and made especially for them. Tuck in a recipe card or a great cloth napkin for color.

I like baskets with a wooden lid and handle, and a woven area on the body of the basket for painting. If the basket is old or discolored you can always spray-paint it, or you can even stain the natural wood.

A favorite fabric can inspire your design. I was inspired by the green and purple grape fabric and a color-coordinated plaid. You can cut out pieces of the fabric to use as lid covers and tie them on with twine or ribbon.

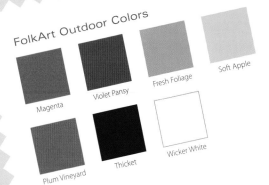

FolkArt Outdoor Colors

Magenta

Violet Pansy

Fresh Foliage

Soft Apple

Plum Vineyard

Thicket

Wicker White

125

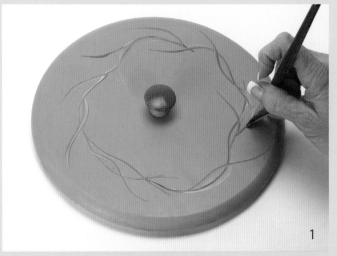

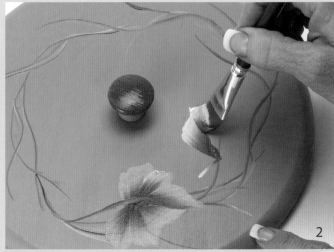

1. Basecoat the wooden lid, the handle and top rim of the basket with Fresh Foliage on a 2-inch (51mm) flat. Use a 3/4-inch (19mm) flat to paint the knob top and the wide woven trim with Plum Vineyard. Double load Soft Apple and Thicket and chisel in a vine around the lid using a 3/4-inch (19mm) flat.

2. Using the same colors and brush and keeping the lighter green to the outside, begin painting the leaves. Start with a V-shape guideline, wiggle the brush out, then come back up to the chisel.

3. Slide back to the center of the leaf.

4. Continue painting the leaf by wiggling out and sliding back in again, but this time make it a little bit smaller.

5. For the third leaf section, wiggle out to the tip and lift to the chisel. Paint the other half of the leaf in the same way.

6. Paint several more large grape leaves to fill in around the lid. Remember to keep the lighter green color to the outside for every leaf. Add a few little one stroke leaves in among the larger leaves using the same brush and colors.

7. Double load a 5/8-inch (16mm) detail painter with Magenta and Wicker White. Pounce the sponge end into each color, touch the lid surface and twist the paint onto the lid. This forms rounded shapes that are shaded and highlighted in one motion.

8. Add some Plum Vineyard to your detail painter and paint some more grapes. Leave some open spaces here and there.

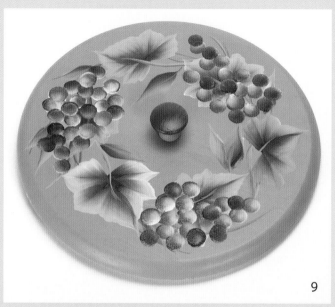

9

9. Pick up some Violet Pansy with the Plum Vineyard on the detail painter and add a few more grapes to fill in. By varying the colors of the grapes, you will create a more natural-looking cluster since grapes don't all ripen at the same time.

10. Finish the lid by outlining the leaves using Fresh Foliage dimensional paint straight from the bottle. Also pull a few stems in among the grape clusters.

11. Paint the leaves on the woven trim of the basket using Soft Apple and Thicket on a 3/4-inch (19mm) flat. Finish by outlining the leaves using Fresh Foliage dimensional paint. Be loose and free with these outlines, and don't forget to pull in the stems. Add a few curlicues here and there if you want.

10

11

12

12. A gift basket wouldn't be complete without a jar of your own homemade soup, sauces or even honey. Paint the outside of the glass canning jar with a matching design after it has been sterilized, filled and sealed. Since you are painting on glass, use the FolkArt Enamels paints and the glass/ceramics brushes. Choose the same or similar colors for the grapes and leaves as you used on the basket. The glass pitcher shown on page 122 would be perfect for serving sparkling white grape juice. Be sure to keep all painting on the outside surfaces.

tropical vase

FolkArt Enamels Paints
- Fresh Foliage
- Thicket
- Burnt Umber
- Yellow Ochre

One Stroke Glass/ Ceramics Brushes
- no. 8 flat
- no. 12 flat

Surface
- Glass vases in many shapes and sizes can be found at any craft supply store, home store, discount or department store. Choose a tall or more vertical vase for this bamboo design.

Are you looking for a great gift idea for a man that is quick to paint and interesting to look at? Try this sophisticated and modern clear glass vase painted with tropical bamboo.

This design works well for people for whom flowers would be inappropriate. The paint colors are subdued and natural looking. And you can fill the vase with almost anything, from glass marbles or rounded river rocks to ferns, ornamental grasses or dried bamboo canes. Signify new beginnings with fresh greenery. Give the gift of a rooted sprig of green bamboo, traditionally a sign of good fortune. Place the vase on a beautiful lacquer tray along with some items from nature for an exotic Asian effect. This special gift is sure to please, especially those hard-to-buy-for men in your life!

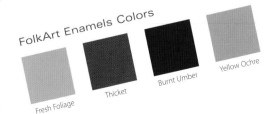

FolkArt Enamels Colors

Fresh Foliage

Thicket

Burnt Umber

Yellow Ochre

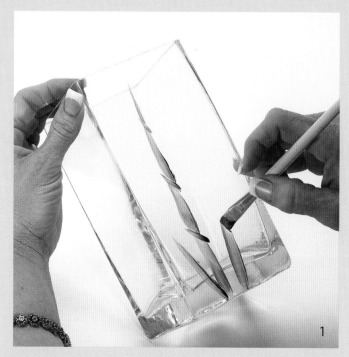

1

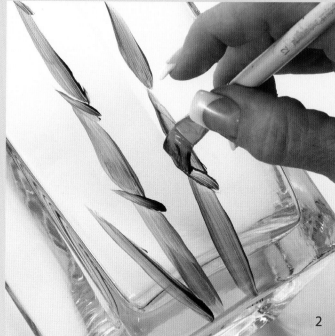

2

1. Clean the glass surface with rubbing alcohol. Take care not to touch the areas you are painting. Double load a no. 12 flat with Burnt Umber and Yellow Ochre and paint the bamboo canes with long, thin leaf strokes (see page 22). I chose a square-sided vase for this design because the flat sides are somewhat easier to paint on than a rounded vase would be.

2. With the same brush and colors, use the chisel edge of the brush to add the cross sections or growth rings of the canes.

3. Double load a no. 12 flat with Burnt Umber and Yellow Ochre and paint the stems using the chisel edge.

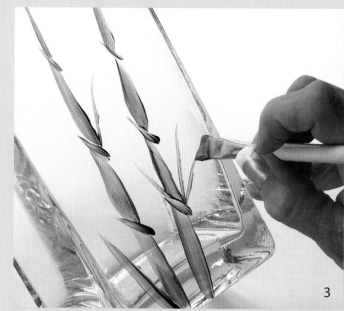

3

4

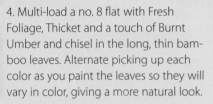

4. Multi-load a no. 8 flat with Fresh Foliage, Thicket and a touch of Burnt Umber and chisel in the long, thin bamboo leaves. Alternate picking up each color as you paint the leaves so they will vary in color, giving a more natural look.

5. Vary the sizes of the leaves, too. Paint more and larger leaves at the bottom, and taper off as you get to the tops of the canes. If you're painting on clear glass as I've done here, I suggest painting only one or two sides of the vase so the design shows up clearly. If you paint on all four sides, it may look confusing. Follow the paint manufacturer's instructions for baking and washing your finished vase.

5

Simple and Beautiful

I like to carry the same theme throughout when I entertain, so here is an idea for an Asian-inspired place setting. Craft and home stores often carry many items made out of woven bamboo, grasses, natural wicker or rattan. Here I'm using woven placemats and matching napkins and rings. The silverware even has faux-bamboo handles. Pull it all together with a delicate floral ribbon and place your bamboo-painted glass vase in the center of the table. The simplicity of this setting will give you and your guests a feeling of serenity and calm, a resting place from the whirlwind of our busy lives.

just for fun!

A simple day at home spending time with friends or family can become the moments we cherish the most. Grilling out in the back yard while the kids or grand-kids play, or taking time off for a short vacation with the family—these are the moments that go by so quickly you can hardly believe it. Help to make those moments even more memorable by painting some-thing special. I love using galvanized metal tubs for ice and sodas when we're grilling on the back deck, and they're easy to paint on with bright summery colors. I also like to make handpainted beach pails for the kids and personalize them with each child's name. They're so easy you can let the kids paint them too. Have fun and enjoy these special times!

FolkArt Enamels and Outdoor Opaque Paints
• See individual items for colors used.

One Stroke Brushes
• nos. 2 and 6 flats
• no. 2 script liner

One Stroke Glass/Ceramics Brushes
• no. 8 flat
• no. 2 script liner
• Small scruffy

Supplies
• FolkArt Enamels Tip-Pen Set
• Clear Medium

Surfaces
• Small 2-inch (5.1cm) or 3-inch (7.6cm) terra cotta pots and various small glass votives can be found at craft supply stores, gardening centers, home stores and discount stores.

candle votives

Candles, flowers and herbs are each great gift ideas. Combine them and you have the perfect gift! You can paint a lot of small terra cotta pots or glass votives quickly, creating gifts that will enchant anyone who receives them.

In this project, I'll show you how to paint a variety of flowering herbs on tiny terra cotta pots used for seedlings, and some wildflowers on little glass votives. These are the perfect size for holding votive candles and will light up your porch or patio in the evening.

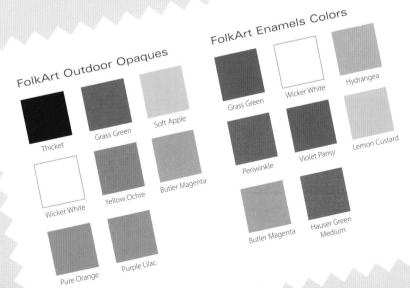

FolkArt Outdoor Opaques

Thicket

Grass Green

Soft Apple

Wicker White

Yellow Ochre

Butler Magenta

Pure Orange

Purple Lilac

FolkArt Enamels Colors

Grass Green

Wicker White

Hydrangea

Periwinkle

Violet Pansy

Lemon Custard

Butler Magenta

Hauser Green Medium

1

2

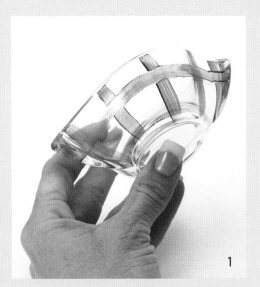

1

2

FolkArt Enamels Paints:

Hauser Green Medium
Wicker White
Hydrangea
Periwinkle
Violet Pansy
Lemon Custard
Butler Magenta

Forget-Me-Nots

1. Clean the glass with rubbing alcohol. Take care not to touch the areas you are painting. Double load a no. 8 flat brush for glass/ceramics with Hauser Green Medium and Wicker White. Paint a diagonal of one-stroke leaves.

2. Double load the no. 8 flat with a lot of Periwinkle and Hydrangea and paint the flowers. Now and then, touch the brush into Violet Pansy and Wicker White, alternating colors for variety. Dot Lemon Custard into the centers with a no. 2 script liner.

Plaid Candle Holder

1. Clean the glass with rubbing alcohol. Don't touch the areas you are painting. With a no. 8 flat and Butler Magenta, paint horizontal and vertical stripes, pressing down on the flat side of the brush to make wide stripes.

2. Load a no. 8 flat with Hydrangea and use the chisel edge of the brush to paint the thin lines of the plaid design.

1

2

FolkArt Enamels Paints:
Wicker White
Butler Magenta
Lemon Custard
School Bus Yellow
Violet Pansy
Grass Green

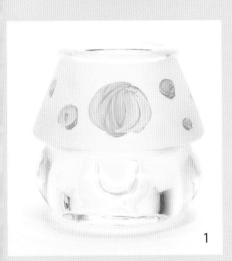

1

2

3

Daisy Votive

1. Clean the glass with rubbing alcohol. Don't touch the areas you are painting. Begin painting the white daisy petals using a no. 8 flat with Wicker White. Pull these little strokes in toward the center. Add more daisies using Butler Magenta wth Wicker White, and Lemon Custard with Wicker White.

2. With the handle end of your brush, dot School Bus Yellow into the daisy centers. Follow the paint manufacturer's instructions for baking and washing your finished pieces.

Pink Roses

1. This lantern-shaped votive has a frosted glass top and a clear glass bottom. Load a no. 8 flat with Violet Pansy and stroke in the base color for the main rose and the buds.

2. Load a no. 2 script liner with Wicker White and paint comma stroke petals. Use Grass Green on a no. 2 script liner for the stems.

3. Double load a no. 8 flat with Grass Green and Wicker White. Finish with small one-stroke leaves.

1

2

FolkArt Enamels Paints:
Wicker White
Hauser Medium Green
Grass Green
Violet Pansy

Blue & White Votive
1. Clean the glass with rubbing alcohol. Take care not to touch the areas you are painting. Load a no. 8 flat with Clear Medium, then sideload with Wicker White (see page 15). Paint two sets of leaves extending outward from the center. The paint should not be opaque—these are subtle background leaves.

2. With the same brush, pick up more Wicker White and paint the flower. Use a no. 2 script liner and Wicker White to add comma strokes and curlicues. Follow the paint manufacturer's instructions for baking and washing your finished votive.

Wisteria Votive
Clean the glass with rubbing alcohol. Try not to touch the areas you are painting. Begin by painting a vine and one-stroke leaves with Hauser Green Medium and Grass Green on a no. 8 flat. Double load a small scruffy with Violet Pansy and Wicker White and pounce on some wisteria. Add a metal Tip-Pen tip onto the bottle of Wicker White and detail the wisteria with tiny lines, curves and squiggles. Follow the paint manufacturer's instructions for baking and washing your finished votive.

FolkArt Outdoor Opaque Paints:

Thicket

Grass Green

Soft Apple

Wicker White

Yellow Ochre

For the blossoms on each terra cotta votive, use a no. 2 flat brush. Most of the flowers are made with little chisel-edge strokes. The key is to pick up enough paint to make the color show up. When painting on terra cotta, you'll find that adding white to the colors really helps make them stand out.

For an informal look, add some freehand stripes around the top rim of each terra cotta pot, alternating between Thicket, Grass Green and Soft Apple in a variety of widths.

1

2

1

2

Shepherd's Purse

1. Double load a no. 6 flat with Thicket and Grass Green. Chisel in the stems and add the ruffled leaves, using the same colors.

2. The flowers of the Shepherd's Purse are little chisel-edge strokes of Wicker White with a dot of Soft Apple in the center of each one.

Agrimony

1. Double load a no. 6 flat with Thicket and Grass Green. Chisel in the stems. Paint the leaves using the same colors with a touch of Soft Apple.

2. Chisel in the yellow blossoms using a no. 2 flat with Yellow Ochre and a touch of Wicker White. The top petals are Soft Apple.

1

2

1

2

FolkArt Outdoor Opaque Paints:
Thicket
Grass Green
Soft Apple
Wicker White
Yellow Ochre
Butler Magenta
Pure Orange

Chives

1. Use a no. 6 flat double loaded with Thicket and Grass Green to chisel in the stems. Add the long, thin leaves using the same colors with a touch of Soft Apple.

2. Chisel in the pink chive blossoms with Wicker White and Butler Magenta. The dried calyxes are Yellow Ochre.

Almond Blossoms

1. Double load a no. 6 flat with Thicket and Grass Green and paint the stems. The leaves and closed buds are the same colors with a touch of Soft Apple.

2. Paint the five-petal flowers with Wicker White and Pure Orange on a no. 2 flat. Dot in the centers with a no. 2 script liner and Pure Orange.

FolkArt Outdoor Opaque Paints:

Thicket
Grass Green
Soft Apple
Wicker White
Purple Lilac

Blue Flax

1. Double load a no. 6 flat with Thicket and Grass Green to chisel in the stems. The leaves are short strokes using the same colors with a touch of Soft Apple.

2. Paint the petals with a no. 2 flat loaded with Purple Lilac and Wicker White. Dot the centers with Grass Green on a no. 2 script liner.

Terra Cotta Saucers

Use some of the designs from your herb pots and paint coordinating saucers. Keep the designs around the edge so they will show when the votive is placed on the saucer.

1. For a saucer with chives, follow the instructions for the Chives votive on page 142.

2. For a saucer with almond blossoms, follow the instructions for the Almond votive on page 142.

1

2

1

2

FolkArt Outdoor
Opaque Paints
- Lemon Custard
- Wicker White
- Soft Apple
- Fresh Foliage
- Hot Pink
- Violet Pansy

FolkArt Outdoor
Dimensional Paints
- Hot Pink
- Fresh Foliage
- Lemon Custard

FolkArt Brushes
- nos. 10 and 12 flats
- 3/4-inch (19mm) flat
- 3/4-inch (19mm) scruffy

Supplies
- FolkArt One Stroke Adhesive
  Background Templates:
  Scallops

Surface
- Galvanized metal tub available at craft supply stores,
  home stores and discount
  stores.

grilling out

Entertaining family and friends is my favorite thing to do, no matter what the season. It's the joy of setting a stage for a wonderful gathering highlighted with beautiful painted pieces. Let the colors and the personality of the season inspire you to create your own design.

Grilling out is always a favorite summer activity. Make your cookout memorable with a galvanized metal tub painted with lemons and inspirational summertime quotes. Fill the tub with ice and your favorite canned or bottled beverages. Lemonade never tasted better than when cooled in this ice-filled tub. Complete the setting with matching flowerpots to hold utensils, napkins or whole lemons for a refreshing and tasty centerpiece.

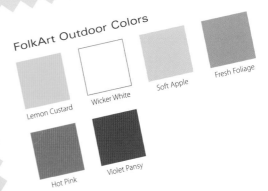

FolkArt Outdoor Colors

Lemon Custard · Wicker White · Soft Apple · Fresh Foliage · Hot Pink · Violet Pansy

1. Apply the adhesive background template with the scallops to the top rim of the galvanized metal tub. Load a 3/4-inch (19mm) scruffy with Wicker White and pounce on the design. Remove the template and fill in the wide white border along the rim.

2. Allow to dry, then add a second coat of Wicker White to the border for better coverage.

3. Double load a 3/4-inch (19mm) flat with Lemon Custard and Wicker White and paint the tip end of the lemon using a C-shaped stroke. Paint the body of the lemon with curving brushstrokes that following the shape, keeping the yellow to the outside edge. Pick up a little Soft Apple on your brush and paint the lower section of the lemon.

4. Continue painting lemons around the tub, as many as you like.

5. To paint the leaves, double load a 3/4-inch (19mm) flat with Fresh Foliage and Soft Apple, and sideload a little Wicker White on the Soft Apple side (see the brush in the photo at top). Begin with the first half of the leaf: wiggle out, then slide to the point as you lift to the chisel (see the smooth-sided leaf demo on page 19).

6. Paint the second half of the leaf, flipping the light edge of the bristles to the inside and sliding out to the point.

7. Continue adding leaves around the tub above and below the lemons.

8. Double load a no. 12 flat with Hot Pink and Wicker White; occasionally pick up a little Violet Pansy on the pink side. Begin the flower petals on the chisel, wiggle out and pull back up to the chisel. Keep the white to the outside edge.

9

10

11

12

9. Dot in the flower centers using Lemon Custard dimensional paint straight from the bottle. Tuck in as many flowers as you like among the lemons and leaves. Outline the leaves using Fresh Foliage dimensional paint. Let these outlines be loose and informal for a fresh and updated look.

10. Sketch the lettering on the white border, then paint with Hot Pink dimensional paint, using the bottle tip to draw the letters.

11. To separate the phrases, add a few green one-stroke leaves to the border using a no. 10 flat double loaded with Fresh Foliage and Soft Apple. Pull in the stems with Soft Apple on the chisel edge of the brush. Finish by shading the letters here and there with Fresh Foliage dimensional paint.

12. Allow the paint to dry for 48 hours before using. The Outdoor paints are durable, weather resistant and easy to care for. Just wash your metal tub with soap and water if needed.

Coordinating Pieces

You can use the same techniques and colors to paint coordinating flower pots. Look for terra cotta pots in different sizes to decorate your outdoor table. I found these pots with a shiny glaze on the lower part in a soft sage green—a perfect background color for painting lemons, leaves and flowers to match the galvanized metal tub.

I wouldn't plant flowers in pots this pretty; instead I would use them on the serving table to hold knives and forks or drinking straws for the kids. Or fill them with whole lemons and place next to a frosty pitcher of lemonade. Mmmm—how refreshing!

Cranberry Cream Cheese Pie

Use either a ready-made graham cracker crust or make one from scratch. Preheat oven to 300°F (150°C).

CRUST:
- 14 squares graham crackers, crushed
- 1/4 cup (59 ml) melted butter or margarine

FILLING:
- 12 oz. (340 g) cream cheese
- 2 eggs or the equivalent of egg substitute
- 3/4 cup (177 ml) granulated sugar
- 2 tsp. (10 ml) vanilla

GLAZE:
- 1/2 cup (118 ml) sour cream
- 2 Tbsp. (30 ml) granulated sugar
- 1/2 tsp. (2.5 ml) vanilla extract

TOPPING
- 3 Tbsp. (45 ml) granulated sugar
- 1 Tbsp. (15 ml) cornstarch
- 1 16-oz. can (454 g) whole cranberry sauce

CRUST:
Combine the crushed graham crackers and melted butter. Press onto the bottom and sides of a 9-inch (23 cm) glass pie dish. Bake for 8 minutes.

FILLING:
Combine the softened cream cheese, eggs, granulated sugar and vanilla in a mixing bowl. Beat on low until mixed, increase speed and beat for 1 minute more or until smooth and light in texture. Pour filling into crumb crust. Bake in preheated oven at 300°F (150°C) for 40 minutes or until it no longer looks wet. Remove from the oven and allow to cool on a rack for 10 minutes.

GLAZE:
Blend together the sour cream, sugar and vanilla. Spread over pie and bake for an additional 5 minutes. Allow to cool completely.

FRUIT TOPPING:
Blend the cornstarch and sugar together. Gradually add the cranberry sauce. Allow the sauce to melt and come to a boil. Cook, stirring constantly, until the mixture is thick, smooth and clear. Cool to room temperature and then spread over the cooled pie. Refrigerate at least 5 hours before serving.

FolkArt Outdoor Paints
- See individual items for colors used.

One Stroke Brushes
- nos. 10, 12 and 16 flats
- 3/4-inch (19mm) flat
- no. 2 script liner

Supplies
- FolkArt One Stroke Adhesive Background Templates: Scallops; and Circles or Dots

Surfaces
- Metal beach pails in light blue or other summery colors are available at home and discount stores. Or look for lidded metal pails used for holding popcorn.
- Wooden palm tree, shell and starfish cutouts available at craft supply stores.

vacation with the kids

D ecorative painting is even more fun when shared with your kids and grandchildren. You will be amazed at how creative kids can be when you hand them a paintbrush and some paint!

These metal pails are great to take along for a fun day at the beach. Let each child come up with his or her own design for their pail so they know which one is theirs to play with. If you're just going to the pool, use them to carry sunscreen and snacks. The Outdoor paint used for these pails is weather-resistant and won't be bothered by wetness.

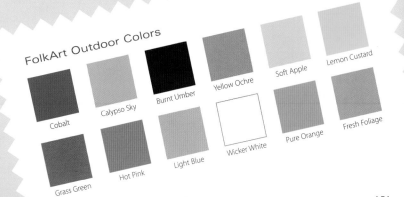

FolkArt Outdoor Colors

Cobalt · Calypso Sky · Burnt Umber · Yellow Ochre · Soft Apple · Lemon Custard · Grass Green · Hot Pink · Light Blue · Wicker White · Pure Orange · Fresh Foliage

Beach Blanket Fun

Kids are always ready for a day at the beach! Let them help with the preparations. They can pack up their newly painted buckets along with their shovel, flip flops and their favorite beach towel or blanket in a large plastic tote bag. You could have a different color for each child!

FolkArt Outdoor Opaque Paints:

Calypso Sky
Cobalt
Soft Apple
Burnt Umber
Yellow Ochre
Grass Green

Stripes and Dots

1. If your metal pail has projections on the sides where the handle attaches, paint them with Calypso Sky. Load a no. 16 flat with Cobalt and paint the wide blue stripes.

2. Space the stripes evenly around the pail.

3. With the same brush and Calypso Sky, add the smaller stripes using the chisel edge of the brush.

4. Paint the circles with a no. 16 flat and Soft Apple.

Wooden Palm Tree Cutout

5. Double load a no. 16 flat with Burnt Umber and Yellow Ochre and paint the sections of the palm tree trunk. Begin at the top and work down, keeping the Burnt Umber side of the brush to the top.

6. Paint the coconuts using the same brush and colors. This time turn the brush so the Burnt Umber is to the bottom.

7. Paint the palm fronds with the same brush loaded with Soft Apple, using a downward stroke. Then pick up some Grass Green and lightly brush over the Soft Apple to shade and separate the leaves.

8. Attach the palm tree to the pail by gluing a small clothes pin to the back of the tree and clipping it on. Or you can attach the palm tree to the pail with a glue that adheres to both wood and metal.

1

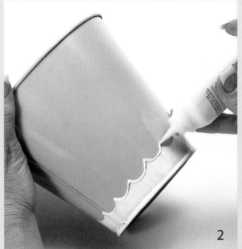

2

3

4

5

Fun & Funky Lettering

1. To create the look of ocean waves around the bottom of the pail, apply the scallop-shaped adhesive background template as shown. Paint a small section using Wicker White and a 3/4-inch (19mm) flat), then lift the template and move it further around and paint another small section. It takes a little longer, but this way the waves will remain level all the way around the bottom of the bucket.

2. Outline the top of the waves with the tip of the Wicker White dimensional paint bottle.

3. Load a no. 10 flat with Wicker White to paint the letters. Alternate between the flat and the chisel to create fun and interesting letters.

4. Embellish some of the letters using the tips of the Cobalt and Fresh Foliage dimensional paint bottles. These wiggly lines and dashes

would be fun for the kids to do with whatever colors they like.

5. Use dimensional paint to add the dots and outlines. The dots are Lemon Custard and the pink swirls are Hot Pink. Finish with a Wicker White outline on each letter and Hot Pink at the tops and bottoms.

FolkArt Outdoor Opaque Paints:
Wicker White
Lemon Custard
Hot Pink

Outdoor Dimensional Paints:
Wicker White
Cobalt
Fresh Foliage
Lemon Custard
Hot Pink

Starfish Cutout

6. Load a no. 16 flat with Wicker White and basecoat the wooden starfish cutout. Paint the pink edges by loading the same brush with Wicker White and sideloading with just a touch of Hot Pink. Follow the shape of the star, keeping the Hot Pink to the edge.

7. Load the same brush with Lemon Custard and chisel in the center of each arm.

8. Use Lemon Custard dimensional paint to add texture dots throughout the center and arms.

9. Finish by attaching the starfish to the pail by gluing a small clothes pin to the back of the star and clipping it on. Or you can attach the starfish to the pail with a glue that adheres to both wood and metal.

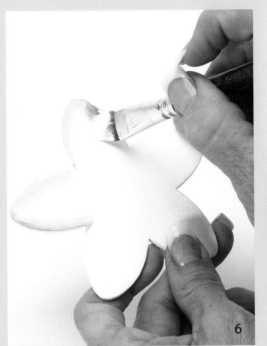

Outdoor Opaque Paints:

Light Blue
Soft Apple
Pure Orange
Lemon Custard
Wicker White
Hot Pink
Grass Green
Cobalt

Outdoor Dimensional Paints:

Wicker White
Hot Pink

Sea Shells

1. To begin the plaid background, load a 3/4-inch (19mm) flat with Light Blue and paint wide horizontal and vertical stripes around the pail and on the lid.

2. Finish the plaid with small stripes of Soft Apple using the chisel edge of the brush.

3. Allow to dry, then use a pencil to lightly sketch the shell design over the plaid. With rubbing alcohol and a paper towel carefully wipe off the plaid colors within the area you are going to paint the shells.

4. Double load Pure Orange and Lemon Custard on a 3/4-inch (19mm) flat and paint C-shaped strokes beginning at the top where the shell is smallest and getting wider toward the bottom. Let each stroke slightly overlap the previous stroke.

5. Double load the same brush with Wicker White and Lemon Custard and paint the mouth of the shell with a large teardrop stroke.

6. Double load a 3/4-inch (19mm) flat with Hot Pink and Wicker White and paint the pink shell using the same techniques.

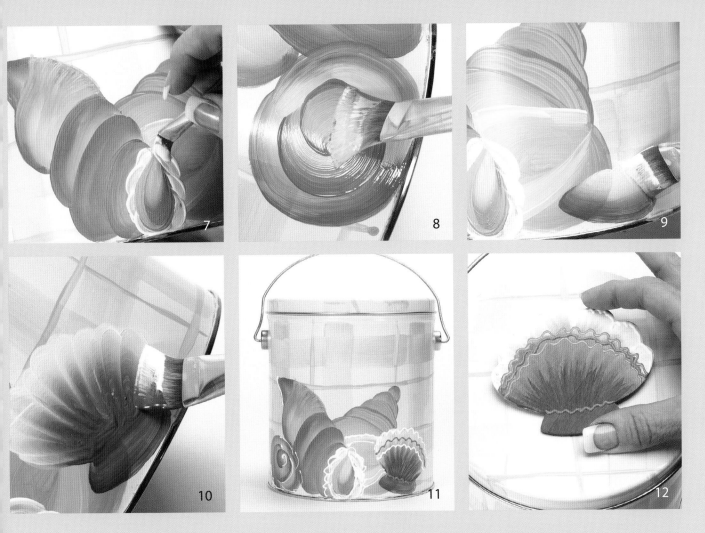

7. Load a no. 2 script liner with Lemon Custard to add a few details across the top of the shell and along the mouth opening; then use a no. 12 flat with Wicker White to paint the ruffled edge.

8. Double load a no. 16 flat with Grass Green and Soft Apple. Paint the green shell using C-shaped strokes in each direction, keeping the darker green to the outside.

9. Double load a 3/4-inch (19mm) flat with Cobalt and Wicker White and paint the bottom section of the blue shell. Begin on the chisel edge, pull down and over, and slide back up to the chisel.

10. Using the same brush and colors, paint the top section of the shell with a wiggle stroke, keeping the white facing out. Chisel in some creases where the two sections of the shell connect.

11. Use the tips of the Wicker White and Hot Pink dimensional paint bottles to embellish the shells with wavy lines.

12. Paint the wooden shell cutout following steps 9 through 11, and attach it to the top of the bucket's lid with a glue that adheres to both wood and metal.

157

Resources

U.S. Retailers

FolkArt paints & mediums;
One-Stroke brushes;
tools listed on page 13:

Plaid Enterprises, Inc.
3225 Westech Dr.
Norcross, GA 30092-3500
USA
Phone: 800-842-4197
www.plaidonline.com

Dewberry Designs, Inc.
365 Citrus Tower Blvd.
Clermont, FL 34711
Phone: 352-394-7344
www.onestroke.com

AmeriColor Soft Gel Paste Food Color:
Julie Motley, Elite Director OSCI
Phone: (360) 893-6916
www.cookiepainting.com

Canadian Retailers

Crafts Canada
120 North Archibald St.
Thunder Bay, ON P7C 3X8
Tel: 888-482-5978
www.craftscanada.ca

Folk Art Enterprises
P.O. Box 1088
Ridgetown, ON, N0P 2C0
Tel: 800-265-9434

Maureen McNaughton Enterprises
RR #2
Belwood, ON, N0B 1J0
Tel: 519-843-5648
www.maureenmcnaughton.com

MacPherson Arts & Crafts
91 Queen St. E.
P.O. Box 1810
St. Mary's, ON, N4X 1C2
Tel: 800-238-6663
www.macphersoncrafts.com

U.K. Retailers

Crafts World (head office)
No. 8 North Street
Guildford
Surrey GU1 4 AF
Tel: 07000 757070

Green & Stone
259 Kings Road
London SW3 5EL
Tel: 020 7352 0837
www.greenandstone.com

Help Desk
HobbyCraft Superstore
The Peel Centre
St. Ann Way
Gloucester
Gloucestershire GL1 5SF
Tel: 01452 424999
www.hobbycraft.co.uk

Index

The best in decorative painting instruction and inspiration is from North Light Books!

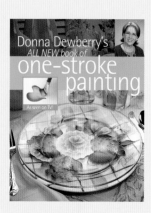

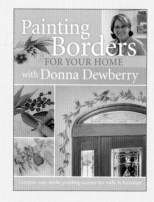

Donna Dewberry's ALL NEW Book of One-Stroke Painting

This is the biggest, most complete guide ever to one-stroke painting! Donna Dewberry's popular, proven one-stroke technique—which lets you color, shade and highlight in a single brushstroke—is a cinch to learn, even if you've never picked up a brush before. This must-have resource features over 200 color photos clearly illustrating every detail of Donna's technique; 12 all-new step-by-step projects for painting on tiles, glassware, floorcloths, cabinets, candles, and more; 5 brand new painting techniques that take you beyond one-stroke; and Donna's foolproof advice for creating attractive designs.
ISBN-13: 978-1-58180-706-6
ISBN-10: 1-58180-706-6
Paperback, 160 pages, #33372

Painting Borders for Your Home with Donna Dewberry

Donna shows you how to use her renowned one-stroke method to create colorful borders that give character and style to every room in your home. Coordinating borders accompany each project, so you can make perfect accessories. With photos showing the borders in actual homes, you'll find the inspiration you need to create masterpieces for walls and furniture throughout your house.
ISBN-13: 978-1-58180-600-7
ISBN-10: 1-58180-600-0
Paperback, 128 pages, #33125

Fantastic Floorcloths You Can Paint in a Day

Want to refresh your home décor without the time and expense of extensive redecorating? Then painting canvas floorcloths is for you! Choose from 23 projects simple enough to create in a few hours. Popular decorative painters Judy Diephouse and Lynne Deptula show you step by step how to paint designs ranging from florals to graphic patterns to holiday motifs, including some especially appropriate for kids' rooms. 12 accessory ideas inspire you to create a coordinated look. *Fantastic Floorcloths You Can Paint in a Day* makes adding creative touches to the home as easy as picking up a paintbrush.
ISBN-13: 978-1-58180-603-8
ISBN-10: 1-58180-603-5
Paperback, 128 pages, #33161

Handpainted Tiles for Your Home

This unique and inspiring book features over 20 fabulous step-by-step projects for transforming ordinary ceramic floor and wall tiles into charming decorative accents. From backsplash tiles and trivets to serving trays and tin wall pockets, you'll find fresh ideas and creative inspiration for all types of personal tastes, including today's favorite decorating themes such as wine country accents, Tuscan-inspired motifs, and French country designs. Tiles of all kinds are inexpensive and easy to find at any home improvement center, and with acrylic paints and sealers, no firing is required!
ISBN-13: 978-1-58180-641-0
ISBN-10: 1-58180-641-8
Paperback, 128 pages, #33227

These books and other fine North Light titles are available at your local arts & crafts retailer, bookstore, or from online suppliers.